MINCE!

100 FABULOUSLY
FRUGAL RECIPES

MINCE!

MITZIE WILSON

100 FABULOUSLY FRUGAL RECIPES

Absolute Press

First published in Great Britain in 2009
by **Absolute Press**
Scarborough House
29 James Street West
Bath BA1 2BT
Phone 44 (0) 1225 316013
Fax 44 (0) 1225 445836
E-mail info@absolutepress.co.uk
Website www.absolutepress.co.uk

Publisher Jon Croft
Commissioning Editor Meg Avent
Designer Matt Inwood
Design Assistant Claire Siggery
Editor Jane Bamforth
Editorial Assistant
Andrea O'Connor
Photography Kate Whitaker
Food Styling Sunil Vijayakar
Props Styling Liz Belton

ISBN: 9781906650018
Printed and bound in England by
Butler Tanner and Dennis Ltd

A note about the text
This book was set using ITC Century
and Serifa. The first Century typeface
was cut in 1894. In 1975, an updated
family of Century typefaces was
designed by Tony Stan for ITC.
The Serifa font was designed by
Adrian Frutiger in 1978.

Thanks
Mince! has been a tasty task! Many
thanks to Meg Avent and Jon Croft for
asking me to do this book and to
Matt Inwood for designing it and seeing
it through to the end.

A big thank you to Sunil Vijayakar
for making brown mince look so
appetising with his superb food styling.
To Liz Belton too, for the lovely props,
and to Kate Whitaker for her beautifully
composed photographs.

This book is for my long-suffering
husband, Dave, and for Angelica and
Georgiana, who have had to eat nothing
but mince for three months. I hope that
one day they will cook these recipes for
themselves.

The author and publisher would also
like to thank the following for giving
permission to use their favourite mince
recipes within this book:

Angela Boggiano
Antony Worral Thompson
www.awtonline.co.uk
Giancarlo Caldesi
www.caldesi.com
Tana Ramsay
www.gordonramsay.com
Rick Stein
www.rickstein.com
Angela Hartnett
www.angelahartnett.co.uk
Mark Leatham
www.merchant-gourmet.com
Phil Vickery
www.vickery.tv

How many times do you pick up a pack of minced meat when you're in the supermarket? Quite often, I'll bet!

But instead of cooking yet another spaghetti Bolognese or shepherd's pie, why not transform it with a few extra ingredients into a spicy curry, a simple hearty pie or a warming main meal soup? Why not sprinkle it onto dough to make some gorgeous spicy flatbreads or try your hand at rolling a meatball?

Mince is magic.

It's the easiest, quickest meat you can cook with and I guarantee that whatever meal with mince you make, your family will be sure to clear their plates!

This book is a collection of invaluable mince recipes; one which celebrates mince in all its forms: beef, lamb, pork, chicken, turkey... even game mince. I hope you will come back to the recipes again and again: mince is that unique staple that feeds families and friends, that can be on the table in minutes with the minimum of fuss, that tastes wonderful... that curious thing that everyone, actually, likes!

There is nothing quite like it, and alongside my favourite recipes for lasagnes, chillis, pasta bakes and burgers, I've included lots of lesser-known wonders, a feast of fresh ideas and a bounty of magical meals from around the world. Enjoy!

Mitzie Wilson, London
March 2009

Minced meat is always great value, but the quality can vary. Mince is generally made from less popular and tougher cuts of meat. The more you pay, the better the meat quality is likely to be and the less fat content it will have. There are, however, no rules about how much meat or fat content there should be in mince, so the mince you get from supermarkets and the mince you get from butchers can vary enormously.

Beef and lamb mince

Minced beef is generally made from the less popular and tougher cuts of meat from the forequarter, including cuts such as shoulder, brisket, flank, neck and shin which are passed through a mincing machine once or twice.

Quality standards

The Quality Standard Mark for beef and lamb is a scheme by EBLEX (English Beef and Lamb Executive) that provides you with high levels of assurance about the meat you buy. The Quality Standard for beef and lamb is the only scheme in the UK to cover eating quality. All beef and lamb carrying the mark is chosen according to a strict selection process to ensure it is succulent and tender. Quality Standard beef and lamb is produced to higher standards than required by law and is inspected at every stage from farm to meat counter. The Quality Standard Mark also tells you where your beef and lamb is from. For example, meat from an animal born, raised and slaughtered in England will carry the Quality Standard Beef or Quality Standard Lamb Mark indicating English origin with the St George's flag. If an animal cannot meet all the criteria, (if it was born in Wales, for example) it will be able to carry the Quality Standard Mark but indicate British origin with the Union flag. The scheme is the only one in the UK to include criteria to improve the eating quality of beef and lamb. Measures such as setting age restrictions to animals entering the supply chain are designed to avoid the resulting meat being tough or dry.

Fat content

The Quality Standard Mince Mark ensures that the mince is 100% beef, with no additives, fillers or added water. The fat content must be no more than 20% for standard beef mince; lean mince contains no more than 10% fat; and extra-lean has no more than 5% fat. Mince that contains more than 20% fat cannot carry the Quality Standard Mark. Steak mince should come from prime cuts of meat and be more tender, so is ideal for burgers. A good indication of the fat content of the mince is to look at the colour. You can see the fat granules in the meat and the redder the meat, the less fat is usually visible.

Pork mince

There are no quality marks for pork mince. It can have quite a high fat content so don't add oil when frying the mince and if a lot of fat should come out when cooked, you can drain the mince through a sieve. Look for lean mince if you prefer.

Turkey and chicken mince

Chicken mince is a lean and healthy choice but not so easy to find in supermarkets. Turkey mince is readily available, very economical and very lean.

Venison and game mince

Venison and game mince is sometimes available in supermarkets, but is more likely to be available in country butchers and specialist suppliers. If you are unable to buy venison or game mince from your local butcher you can order it on line. YorkshireGame.co.uk and it's partner company blackface.co.uk will deliver any game or venison cut you could need, and the quality is superb. Venison is a very lean meat and so venison mince tends to be a little dry, it is a good idea to mix it with good quality, fatty beef mince to add a little fat content. Game mince can be a mixture of meats so check with your supplier before you buy.

How to cook mince

Standard beef, lamb, pork and venison mince has around 20% fat content so I prefer not to use oil or extra fat when cooking as it will fry in its own fat. If you find that a lot of oil comes out of the mince, drain some of it off, or skim it off once it has cooked and cooled. Lean mince, chicken and turkey mince may need to be fried in a little oil, but keep it to a minimum or you are defeating the object!

Always get the pan hot before you fry mince, and stir it while frying to break up the clumps. Generally, mince needs only 10 minutes over a high heat – until all the meat has turned brown – to cook. Further cooking, however, helps to make the mince more tender, and that usually means simmering for at least another 10–30 minutes. Longer cooking helps meld all the flavours together and will make it even more succulent.

Making burgers

It's a good idea when making homemade burgers to make them as flat as possible and not too thick. The thicker they are the longer they will take to cook in the centre, whilst the outside becomes blacker and blacker. Try to chill burgers for 30 minutes in the fridge before cooking to help them firm up.

Cooking burgers

All burgers should be cooked until no longer pink in the centre – use a knife to pierce the centre and the juices should run clear. A good test is to pierce the centre of the burger with a knife, count to 3, then place the tip of the knife against your wrist, if it is hot to the touch the burger is cooked. Better still, cut one burger in half and check that it is no longer pink.

Avoid over-cooking home made burgers as they have a tendency to be dry, and remember to leave them to rest for 5 minutes before serving so that the meat relaxes and the juices distribute evenly throughout.

Beef burgers can be served medium to well done, but chicken, turkey, lamb and pork burgers must be cooked thoroughly.

Burger cooking times

For $1\frac{1}{2}$–2cm thick under a hot grill or barbecue:
Beef burgers
3–4 minutes each side
Chicken/turkey/lamb pork burgers
5–6 minutes each side

If you are cooking or barbecueing lots of burgers for a crowd, fry them for 2–3 minutes on each side then place in a very hot oven for a further 10 minutes for medium-cooked.

Making meatballs

Having gone to the trouble of making meatballs, it's extremely disappointing to discover that they taste bland when served up. Avoid the scenario altogether by frying just a little bit of your mixture in hot oil ahead of cooking the rest. That way you get to taste a sample of the cooked mixture and can make minor – or major! – adjustments to flavour and seasoning as desired.

To freeze mince

You should freeze raw mince on the day of purchase. Never re-freeze defrosted raw mince. Cooked mince can be chilled and reheated the next day and freezes beautifully. That means you can batch-cook to your heart's content! You can save yourself time and money cooking like this: stretching a batch of cooked mince over two nights or storing away readymade meals for those busy weekday evenings when the last thing you want to do is set up in the kitchen for an hour. If you are making meals in bulk, freeze them in plastic bags or sealed freezer containers for up to 3 months. The night before you plan to eat them, defrost them in the fridge. Mince must always be reheated thoroughly; the centre of the dish should reach boiling point for at least 10 minutes.

Freezing burgers

Uncooked burgers can easily be frozen. Freeze them in a single layer on a tray if possible, then pack into a plastic freezer bag and seal tightly. Alternatively, layer the burgers with squares of baking parchment in-between if you don't have the room to lay them flat. Freeze burgers for up to 3 months. If using strong flavours such as garlic and curry spices they may be better if frozen for only 1 month, as the flavours can develop too strongly after this time. Burgers should be defosted overnight in the fridge. I don't like cooking homemade burgers from frozen as it takes too long to cook the meat through to the centre.

HUNGRY HOARDS

Our love affair with mince begins as a toddler, when spaghetti Bolognese and cottage pie are some of the first solid foods we are introduced to. Mince is easy to eat, easy to cook and economical too, so it's no wonder we continue to cook it in one form or another almost every week. Here you'll find all your staple mince meals – the dishes you'll turn to most often knowing your families will enjoy them. But we all need a little help to keep us inspired in the kitchen (and claim a few well deserved compliments from the family now and again), so I hope you'll find plenty of new ideas to try here too, and that you end up with clean plates all round!

Everyday mince

This straightforward everyday meal will become a regular favourite. I make a big batch of this sauce (double or treble the quantities here) and freeze it in portions for later use. It is perfect comfort food to use for cottage pie, or to serve with mash, or pasta. If you want to make it richer use red wine instead of stock. If you want more vegetables in it add chopped mushrooms, tomatoes or courgettes or – in the winter – swede or parsnip.

Serves 6–8 | Takes 15 minutes to make, 30 minutes to cook

500g minced lamb or beef
2 medium onions chopped
1 clove garlic, crushed
2 carrots, diced
2 tbsp tomato purée
1 tbsp plain flour
300ml lamb stock
salt and freshly ground black pepper

Dry-fry the minced lamb and onion in a large pan over a high heat until the onion has softened and the meat has browned. Add the garlic, fry for 1–2 minutes then add the carrots, tomato purée and sprinkle over the flour. Cook for a further 2–3 minutes until the flour has been absorbed, then pour over the stock, stirring well until thickened. Lower the heat and simmer the mince for 30 minutes. Taste and adjust seasoning.

Freeze for up to 3 months. Defrost overnight and reheat thoroughly.

Million-vegetable mince

This is a brilliant way of getting children to eat vegetables; just finely chop any vegetables you have in the food processor and then disguise them by cooking with the mince. Cook the lot in a tomato-flavoured sauce and serve with spaghetti and your kids will never know they're eating so healthily.

**Serves 6 | Takes 15 minutes
to make, 30 minutes to cook**

**2 medium onions
2 carrots
1 red pepper, deseeded
2 courgettes
150g mushrooms
500g minced lamb or beef
1 clove garlic, crushed
2 tbsp tomato purée
1 tsp dried oregano
300ml lamb stock
400g can chopped tomatoes
salt and freshly ground black
   pepper**

Chop the onions, carrots, pepper and courgettes into chunks and place in a food processor with the mushrooms. Whizz until quite finely chopped. Place the mince in a large saucepan and fry until the meat has browned all over.

Add all the chopped vegetables, garlic, tomato purée and oregano. Cook for a further 5–10 minutes stirring well, then pour over the stock and canned tomatoes. Season well, bring to the boil, then lower the heat and simmer the mince for 30 minutes. Taste and adjust seasoning.

**Freeze for up to 3 months.
Defrost overnight and reheat
thoroughly.**

Cottage pie

This is the classic family favourite. A shepherd's pie is made with lamb in exactly the same way. Add cooked carrots, parsnips or cabbage to the mash if liked, and top with grated cheese too to make for an even more delicious dish.

Serves 4 | Takes 30 minutes to make, 30 minutes to cook

500g minced beef
1 onion, finely chopped
1 carrot, diced
1 tbsp tomato purée
300ml beef stock
1½ tbsp Worcestershire sauce
700g floury potatoes
100ml milk
50g butter
salt and freshly ground black pepper

Fry the minced beef, onion and carrot in a medium pan for about 5 minutes until browned. Add the tomato purée, beef stock and Worcestershire sauce, bring to the boil then cover and simmer for 20 minutes.

Set the oven to 180°C/160°C fan/gas 4.

Meanwhile, boil the potatoes in lightly salted water for 15–20 minutes or until tender. Drain well. Add the milk and butter, season and mash well. Pour the mince into a 2-litre baking dish and top with the mashed potato. Bake for 20–30 minutes until golden brown and bubbling.

This can be made a day in advance and reheated thoroughly until piping hot in the centre. It can also be frozen although the mashed potato may be a little watery when defrosted, so if planning to freeze it, add less milk to the mixture. Freeze for up to 3 months. Defrost overnight in the fridge before reheating for 45 minutes–1 hour or until piping hot in the centre.

Meat and tatties

The juices from the minced lamb help to cook the layers of potato, so you end up with a lovely thick moist dish. While this might not be the most glamorous of meals, it's certainly one of the most comforting!

Serves 6 | Takes 20 minutes
to make, 45 minutes to cook

1kg potatoes
2 large onions
2 tbsp sunflower oil
500g minced lamb or beef
1 clove garlic, crushed
1 carrot, diced
100g swede, diced
2 tbsp tomato purée
1 sprig rosemary, leaves stripped
  and chopped
1 tbsp plain flour
300ml lamb stock
salt and freshly ground black
  pepper
25g butter

Peel the potatoes and slice as thinly as possible. Peel and slice the onions. Heat the oil in a pan and add the onions. Cook without browning for 5 minutes until transparent. In a separate pan dry-fry the mince for 5 minutes until browned. Add the garlic, carrot, swede, tomato purée and rosemary and cook for 2–3 minutes then add the flour and stir well. Gradually add the stock stirring well until thickened. Season well and bring to the boil.

Set the oven to 190°C/170°C fan/gas 6.

Layer half of the sliced potatoes and half the onions in the base of a shallow 2-litre baking dish and top with the meat sauce. Top with another layer of onions and potatoes. Season well. Cook on the hob over a low heat for 5 minutes, then dot with the butter, cover with a tight fitting lid and transfer to the oven for 30 minutes until the potatoes are tender. Remove the lid and cook for a further 15 minutes until the potatoes are tender and golden.

Not suitable for freezing.

Shepherd's pie with cheesy parsnip mash

This mash uses lots of traditional British vegetables and is delicious on its own or when used in this twist on a classic cottage pie. You can of course top it with plain mashed potatoes if you prefer.

Serves 4–6 | Takes 1 hour to make, 25–30 minutes to cook

500g minced lamb
2 onions, finely chopped
3 carrots, finely chopped
1/2 swede, finely chopped
250g mushrooms, finely chopped
2 tbsp plain flour
2 lamb stock cubes, crumbled
2 tbsp Worcestershire sauce
2 tbsp tomato purée
salt and freshly ground black pepper

For the topping
1kg potatoes
500g parsnips
100ml milk
50g butter
50g Parmesan cheese, grated

Dry-fry the lamb mince and onions for 5 minutes until the mince is browned. Add the remaining vegetables, fry for another 5 minutes, then sprinkle over the flour and crumbled stock cubes. Cook for a few minutes, then pour in 600ml boiling water and stir to combine. Add the Worcestershire sauce and tomato purée, then taste and season. Simmer for 40 minutes.

Set the oven to 220°C/200°C fan /gas 7. Meanwhile, make the topping. Peel and quarter the vegetables. Put the potatoes into a large pan of lightly salted water, bring to the boil and cook for 7 minutes. Add the parsnips and cook until both the potatoes and parsnips are tender. Drain, then mash with the milk, butter and Parmesan. Season. Use a fork to spread the mash over the mince. Cook in the oven for 25–30 minutes, until piping hot.

Freeze for up to 3 months, although the mashed potato may become a little watery when frozen so use less milk if you intend to freeze it. Defrost overnight in the fridge and reheat for 45 minutes–1 hour or until piping hot in the centre.

Traditional meat and potato pie

Anyone over the age of 50 will recognise this as the staple of old school dinners. Rich, comforting and very tasty, as well as economical. This recipe is adapted from my friend Angela Boggiano's book, *Pie* (Mitchell Beazley) – a fantastic collection of the best pie recipes ever. Readymade shortcrust will save you time, but for authentic taste nothing quite beats homemade crisp, yet-crumbly, pastry. You can add any number of other vegetables to make the meat stretch even further, but most importantly, don't forget to serve it with peas and lashings of hot gravy!

Serves 6 | Takes 50 minutes to make plus chilling time, 30 minutes to cook

For the filling
1 onion, finely diced
2 carrots, diced
450g minced beef
2 tbsp tomato ketchup
1 tbsp Worcestershire sauce
2 tsp Marmite or other yeast extract
1$^1/_2$ tbsp plain flour
$^1/_2$ tsp salt
freshly ground black pepper
1 large baking potato, finely diced

For the pastry
300g plain flour, plus a little for dusting
salt
75g butter
75g lard or vegetable fat
5–6 tbsp water
1 tbsp milk, to glaze

mashed potatoes, peas and gravy, to serve

Dry-fry the onion, carrots and beef together in a medium saucepan over a high heat until browned, then reduce the heat and add the tomato ketchup, Worcestershire sauce, Marmite, flour and seasoning. Stir well and cook for 1 minute then add the diced potato, pour over 150ml water and bring to the boil. Reduce the heat, cover and simmer for 15 minutes. Allow to cool completely.

Make the pastry. Place the flour in a bowl with a pinch of salt. Cut the butter and lard into small pieces and rub between your fingertips until the mixture resembles fine breadcrumbs. Add 5 tablespoons of cold water and form the mixture into a ball, adding a little more water if necessary. Chill for 30 minutes if possible.

Heat the oven to 200°C/180°C fan/gas 6. Dust a work surface with flour and roll out two thirds of the pastry to a square large enough to cover the base and sides of a 20cm-square, 4cm-deep cake tin. Add the cooled mince, then roll out the remaining pastry for the lid. Dampen the edge of the pastry then place the pastry lid on top of the pie and press the edges well to seal. Use a fork to pierce the top several times and brush with milk. Bake for 30 minutes until golden brown. Serve hot with mashed potatoes, peas and gravy.

Freeze for up to 3 months. Defrost overnight in the fridge then reheat thoroughly.

Phil Vickery's really easy mince hotpot with mushrooms

I worked with Phil Vickery at one of the very first *Good Food* shows when I was editor of *Good Food* magazine. I was preparing food for my own demonstration when Phil came over and very kindly offered to help me make tonnes of caramel for the *croquembouche* I was creating... we've kept in touch ever since. The shows were exhausting but all the chefs were under one roof and that enabled us to have the most amazing thank you dinner for them at the show. Quite how anyone got up the next morning to demonstrate to the crowds I'll never know! I think we all survived on adrenalin for those four days, but there were always great tales to be told afterwards! This is a really homely supper that I'm sure Phil, Fern and their family love.

Serves 6–8 | Takes 15 minutes to make, 50 minutes to cook

4 tbsp vegetable oil
2 small onions, chopped
2 cloves garlic, chopped
200g mushrooms, thickly sliced
500g minced beef
1 tbsp plain flour
400g can chopped tomatoes with herbs
1 small pot of growing basil, leaves trimmed and roughly chopped
1 level tbsp beef granules
3 tbsp brown sauce
5 large potatoes, chopped into 3cm chunks
salt and freshly ground black pepper
2 tbsp vegetable oil

Set the oven to 200°C/180°fan/gas 6.

Heat 2 tablespoons of the vegetable oil in a 2-litre flameproof casserole dish. Add the chopped onions, garlic and mushrooms. Cook over a high heat for 10 minutes.

Add the mince, break up well, and cook until it changes colour from red to light brown. Stir in the flour, tomatoes, basil, beef granules, brown sauce and mix really well.

Toss the chopped potatoes in a large bowl with a little salt, pepper and the remaining vegetable oil. Pile the potatoes onto the mixture, cover and bake in the oven for 30 minutes. At this point, remove the lid and cook for a further 20 minutes to brown the potatoes nicely. Serve.

Freeze for up to 3 months. Defrost overnight in the fridge and reheat for 45 minutes–1 hour or until piping hot in the centre.

Beef and beans with oaty cheese crumble

This is delicious, economical, filling family food. The cheesy oat crumble works really well with the mince. If you prefer, you can leave out the beans and add extra vegetables instead, and you can add pumpkin and sunflower seeds to the crumble for extra crunch too.

Serves 6 | Takes 20 minutes to make, 20 minutes to cook

500g minced beef
1 onion, finely chopped
2 tbsp tomato ketchup
2 tbsp brown sauce
400g can baked beans
salt and freshly ground black pepper

For the crumble
175g plain flour
75g porridge oats
50g butter, cubed
75g Cheddar cheese, grated
pinch English mustard powder
salt and freshly ground black pepper

Dry-fry the beef and onion together in a medium saucepan for about 5 minutes until browned, add the tomato ketchup, brown sauce, baked beans, $\frac{1}{2}$ teaspoon of salt and plenty of black pepper. Add about 150ml boiling water, if necessary, to give a moist but not too sloppy gravy. Bring to the boil then reduce the heat and simmer for 15 minutes.

Set the oven to 200°C/180°C fan/gas 6.

To make the crumble, place the flour and oats into a mixing bowl, add the butter, and rub it into the flour with your fingertips until the mixture resembles breadcrumbs. Stir in the cheese, mustard and salt and pepper. Sprinkle the crumble over the mince and bake for 20 minutes until golden.

Not suitable for freezing as the crumble goes soggy!

Spaghetti Bolognese

To help reduce the fat content when cooking with mince, I usually dry-fry the mince and onion, but in this instance it is important to fry the bacon and vegetables to get the most from their flavour. This is a standard Bolognese recipe, but you can add sliced mushrooms if liked, use pancetta instead of bacon, and use either all red wine or all beef stock depending on who you are catering for. A richer version, although not so popular with children, is to fry 100g of chopped chicken livers and add them to the mince.

Serves 6 | Takes 15 minutes to make, 20 minutes to cook

1 tbsp vegetable oil
3–4 rashers streaky bacon, chopped
1 onion, finely chopped
2 carrots coarsely grated or very finely diced
1 stick celery
2 cloves garlic, crushed
500g minced beef
1 tsp dried oregano
400g can tomatoes
2 tbsp tomato purée
150ml full bodied red wine
150ml beef stock
salt and freshly ground black pepper
spaghetti, to serve
grated Parmesan and chopped parsley, to serve (optional)

Heat the oil in a medium to large saucepan and fry the bacon, onion, carrots and celery over a medium heat until the bacon is translucent and tender. Add the garlic and fry for another minute or so, then tip the mixture out of the pan and set aside.

Add the mince to the pan and fry until browned and crumbly. Return the vegetables to the pan and add the oregano, tomatoes, tomato purée and red wine and stock. Bring to the boil and then lower the heat, cover and simmer for 20 minutes until tender.

Taste and adjust the seasoning, and serve with cooked spaghetti and grated Parmesan and chopped parsley, if liked.

Freeze for up to 3 months. Defrost overnight in the fridge and reheat thoroughly.

Braised faggots with onion gravy

Brains Faggots (a brand name not the component ingredient!) were really popular when I was growing up, but they have gone out of fashion. These days it's rare to find faggots in supermarkets or on restaurant menus; a great shame as they are a rich, hearty and economical meal. Perhaps it's time to rediscover them for your family? I've adapted this from a recipe from the English Beef and Lamb Executive, who know a thing or two aboout cooking meat!

Serves 6 | Takes 20 minutes to make, 1 hour 20 minutes to cook

100g white or wholemeal bread, from a crusty loaf
2 cloves garlic, crushed
100g lamb's liver
100g streaky bacon
1 small onion
1 tbsp chopped fresh parsley
leaves from 2 sprigs thyme
4–5 sage leaves
500g minced beef
2 tsp English mustard

For the onion gravy
1 tbsp rapeseed oil
2 large onions, finely chopped
1 tbsp plain flour
300ml brown ale
600ml beef stock
2 tsp Worcestershire sauce
2 tsp mixed dried herbs

Tear up the bread and place in a food processor with the garlic, liver, bacon, onion and herbs. Whizz until finely chopped. Add the beef and mustard and whizz again to mix everything together. Shape the mixture into about 12 golf-sized balls and place in a roasting tin. Chill while making the onion gravy.

Set the oven to 180°C/160°C fan/gas 4.

Heat the oil in a medium sized pan and fry the onions for 4–5 minutes until softened and golden brown. Add the flour and cook for 1 minute, then gradually pour on the ale and stock, stirring until smooth and thickened. Add the Worcestershire sauce and herbs, taste and season if necessary. Pour over the meat balls, cover with foil and place in the oven. Roast for $1\frac{1}{2}$ hours then remove the foil and return to the oven for a further 15–20 minutes. Serve with mashed potatoes and green vegetables.

Freeze for up to 3 months. Defrost overnight and reheat thoroughly.

Rumbledethumps pie

This is a lovely autumnal dish and a great way to get the family to eat more veg. Rumbledethumps is a traditional dish from the Scottish borders – simply potato, swede, cabbage and cheese when served as a side dish, but use it to top minced beef and you have the perfect comforting supper.

Serves 6 | Takes 20 minutes to make, 20 minutes to cook

650g potatoes
$^1/_2$ swede
$^1/_4$ small Savoy cabbage, shredded
50g butter
500g minced beef
1 onion
1 tbsp Worcestershire sauce
2 tbsp tomato purée
1 tbsp plain flour
1 beef stock cube
50g Cheddar cheese, grated
salt

Peel and quarter the potatoes and peel and chop the swede into 2cm cubes. Cook both together in lightly salted boiling water for about 15 minutes then add the cabbage and cook for a further 3–4 minutes. Drain well then add the butter to the pan and lightly break up the potatoes with a fork.

Meanwhile, dry-fry the minced beef and onion in a medium pan until the meat is browned and the onion is beginning to soften. Add the Worcestershire sauce, tomato purée and flour and stir well. Dissolve the stock cube in 350ml boiling water and add to the meat, stirring well until thickened. Simmer for 10 minutes.

Set the oven to 180°C/160°C fan/gas 4. Pour the meat mixture into a 2-litre ovenproof baking dish and pile the potato mixture on top. Scatter with cheese and bake for 20 minutes until golden and bubbling.

Freeze for up to 3 months. Defrost overnight and reheat for 45 minutes–1 hour or until piping hot in the centre.

Deer stalker's pie

This is a variation on cottage pie, using game mince and bubble and squeak. Game mince has quite a strong flavour but the vegetables help to sweeten it. For a richer, more grown-up version, replace half of the beef stock with red wine. Sometimes, I also sprinkle a few pumpkin, sunflower and sesame seeds on top for a bit of extra crunch.

Serves 4 | Takes 20 minutes to make, 1 hour to cook

**500g minced game
2 onions, finely chopped
1 parsnip, diced
2 carrots, diced
1 cooked beetroot, diced
1 tbsp chopped fresh parsley
2 tbsp tomato purée
1 tbsp plain flour
400ml beef stock
700g floury potatoes
250g Savoy cabbage, shredded or
   sprouts, roughly chopped
100ml milk
50g butter
salt and freshly ground black
   pepper**

Dry-fry the minced game in a large pan for about 10 minutes until browned all over. Add the onion, parsnip, carrots and beetroot and fry for a further 5 minutes. Stir in the parsley, tomato pureé and flour, stir well, then stir in the beef stock. Bring to the boil then reduce the heat, cover and simmer for 30 minutes.

Meanwhile boil the potatoes in lightly salted water for 15–20 minutes or until tender.

Set the oven to 200°C/180°fan/gas 6.

Boil the cabbage or sprouts for 5 minutes or until tender but still with a little bite. Drain the potatoes and the cabbage or sprouts. Add the milk and butter to the potatoes, season and mash well. Add the cabbage or sprouts and mix well. Pour the mince into a 2-litre baking dish and top with the bubble and squeak. Bake for 20–30 minutes until golden brown and bubbling.

This can be made in advance and baked the next day or frozen before baking. Freeze for up to 1 month only, defrost overnight in the fridge and bake for about 45 minutes–1 hour or until piping hot in the centre.

Beef in red wine with Stilton and rosemary scones

A delicious, warming and very filling dish to enjoy for Sunday lunch or on a cold winter's night. You could bake the scones on a baking tray if you prefer but the fact that they soak up some of the meaty juices is what makes them so tasty.

Serves 8 | Takes 30 minutes to make, 20 minutes to cook

1kg steak mince
3 carrots, finely diced
1 large onion, finely chopped
3 cloves garlic, finely chopped
1 tsp dried chilli flakes
1 tbsp flour
4 tbsp tomato purée
600ml full bodied red wine
2 tbsp chopped fresh parsley
2 sprigs fresh rosemary, leaves chopped

For the scones
250g plain flour
2 tsp baking powder
50g butter
75g Stilton or full flavoured blue cheese
1 sprig fresh rosemary
salt and plenty of freshly ground black pepper
1/2 tsp English mustard powder
150ml milk

Dry-fry the mince, carrot and onion in a large flameproof casserole for 5–10 minutes until browned. Add the garlic and fry for 2 minutes then add the chilli flakes, flour and tomato purée. Stir for 1–2 minutes then gradually pour on the red wine, stirring until smooth and thickened. Add the herbs, cover and simmer for 10 minutes while making the scones.

Set the oven to 220°C/200°C fan/gas 7.

Mix the flour and baking powder together then add the butter and rub it into the flour with your fingertips until it looks like breadcrumbs. Grate or finely crumble the cheese into the mixture. Strip off the rosemary leaves and snip into the flour with the seasoning and mustard powder. Add the milk and stir to make a soft dough. Turn out onto a floured work surface and pat smooth but do not knead or the mixture will be tough. Using a pastry cutter cut 8 x 7cm scones. Place on top of the hot mince mixture and cook in the oven for 15–20 minutes until the scones are risen and golden brown.

Freeze the mince only, for up to 3 months. Defrost overnight and reheat thoroughly. Make and add the scones when the mince has boiled for about 10 minutes.

Cheat's chicken curry

A tin of tomatoes and some curry paste are all you need to turn mince into an easy curry. The yoghurt makes it creamy and tangy too. Add lots of vegetables if you want to stretch the meat further too.

Serves 6 | Takes 15 minutes to make, 30 minutes to cook

**1 tbsp sunflower oil
500g minced chicken or turkey
2 onions, sliced
2 tbsp curry paste
400g can chopped tomatoes
100g red lentils
2 handfuls fresh spinach
4 tbsp natural Greek yoghurt**

Heat the oil in a medium pan and fry the mince and onions for 5 minutes until the mince is browned all over and the onion is getting tender. Add the curry paste and cook for 1–2 minutes, then pour over the canned tomatoes and sprinkle over the lentils. Add boiling water to the empty can and pour the water into the pan. Bring to the boil and boil rapidly for 10 minutes then reduce the heat and simmer for 15–20 minutes until the lentils are soft.

Just before serving, stir in the spinach and yoghurt. Heat through and serve with boiled rice.

Freeze for up to 1 month. Defrost overnight in the fridge and reheat thoroughly.

Suet-crusted Teviotdale pie

Originating in the Scottish Borders, this is real thrifty, hearty, comfort food, which makes a little mince go a long way. Traditionally made very plainly, I've added herbs to the crust to make it more tasty and added vegetables to the mince to make it a complete meal.

Serves 6 | Takes 25 minute to make, 35 minutes to cook

500g lean minced beef
1 onion, chopped
1 teaspoon plain flour
1 large carrot, diced
300ml beef stock
1 tbsp Worcestershire sauce
225g self-raising flour
25g cornflour
75g shredded suet
$\frac{1}{2}$ tsp mustard powder
leaves from a few sprigs of thyme
300ml milk
salt and freshly ground black
    pepper

Set the oven to 180°C /160°fan/Gas 4.

Dry-fry the mince and onion in a 1.5-litre flameproof casserole for about 5–10 minutes until browned. Sprinkle over the flour, cook for 1 minute then add the carrot, stock and Worcestershire sauce.

Put the flour, cornflour and suet in a bowl, then stir in the mustard powder, thyme and plenty of seasoning. Gradually stir in the milk to form a thick batter. Pour it over the mince mixture and bake for 30–35 minutes until risen and browned. Serve with a green vegetable.

Not suitable for freezing as the crust will be soggy and won't be nearly as nice as when freshly baked.

BEEF

Pork and pistachio pâté

I had to find room for this simple, rustic, country-style pâté. It makes for a lovely laid-back lunch, when served with crusty bread and chutney.

Serves 8 | Takes 25 minutes to make, 1 hour to cook

1 tbsp olive oil
175g streaky bacon
100g chicken livers
500g minced pork
75ml good red wine
1 tbsp whisky or brandy
5 juniper berries, crushed
1 tbsp chopped fresh parsley
leaves from 1 sprig thyme
50g shelled pistachio nuts
**$\frac{1}{2}$ tsp salt and freshly ground
   black pepper**
crusty bread and chutney, to serve

Brush a 500g loaf tin with a little of the oil. Place each bacon rasher on a chopping board and stretch them with the back of a knife, then lay the bacon rashers across the tin to line it completely, allowing the bacon to hang over the sides.

Heat the remaining oil in a frying pan and fry the chicken livers for 2 minutes until just browned. Allow to cool a little then roughly chop.

Mix the pork mince with the red wine, whisky or brandy, juniper and herbs, then add the chicken livers and pistachios, season and mix well. Pack into the bacon-lined tin and fold the bacon over the top.

Set the oven to 180°C/160°C fan/gas 4. Cover the terrine with a layer of baking parchment and a layer of foil and seal the edges well. Place the terrine in a roasting tin half filled with hot water. Bake for 1 hour or until firm and cooked through.

Leave to cool completely in the tin, then place a bag of sugar or weights on top and place in the fridge overnight until completely cold and set. Turn out and serve sliced with bread and chutney.

Store in the fridge for up to 3 days. Not suitable for freezing.

Pork and bacon pie with cauliflower cheese mash

Pork and leeks are a classic combination. Add cheesy cauliflower mash and you have a great family pie full of flavour and vegetables that even children will tuck into. It's a very filling dish; you can omit the pastry if you prefer.

Serves 6 | Takes 50 minutes
to make, 25 minutes to cook

For the mash
850g potatoes, cut into chunks
300g cauliflower florets
75ml semi-skimmed milk
50g mature Cheddar cheese, grated
2 tsp wholegrain mustard

For the pork and bacon filling
1 onion, chopped
500g minced pork
150g back bacon, snipped
2 leeks, halved, rinsed and thinly sliced
2 tbsp plain flour
200–300ml dry cider
1 tsp wholegrain mustard
500g shortcrust pastry
salt and freshly ground black pepper

You will need 6 18cm individual pie dishes or a 1.5-litre baking dish

Boil the potatoes in lightly salted water for about 20 minutes until cooked. Boil the cauliflower in water for about 6 minutes until just tender. Drain and mash the potatoes with the milk, cheese, mustard and seasoning. Drain the cauliflower and, with a fork, begin to break it up just a little as you lightly fold it into the mash.

While the potatoes are boiling, cook the filling. Dry-fry the onion, pork and bacon in a large pan for 5–6 minutes then add the leeks. Fry for a further 3–4 minutes then add the flour and stir well until thickened.

Gradually pour on the cider and up to 100ml water if needed, to make a thick creamy sauce. Bring to the boil, then reduce the heat and simmer for 10 minutes. Add the mustard, taste and season if necessary and allow to cool.

Set oven at 220°C/200°C fan/gas 7.

Roll pastry out on a floured board until large enough to line the pie dish (cut the pastry into 6 equal pieces if using 6 individual pie dishes). Drape into the pie dish, trim the edge. Spoon the pork into the centre and pile the mash on top. Crimp the pastry edge if liked. Bake for 25–35 minutes for the individual pie, 45 minutes for the large pie until golden brown and bubbling. Serve hot.

This can be assembled a day in advance and baked the next day until piping hot in the centre. It can also be frozen before baking although the mashed potato may be a little watery when defrosted, so if planning to freeze it, add less milk to the mixture. Freeze for up to 1 month only. Defrost overnight in the fridge before reheating thoroughly.

Venison, cranberry and chestnut casserole

Lots of my favourite autumnal flavours in one dish. This is a rich and hearty dish ideal for entertaining. Serve as a casserole (add dumplings or herb scones – see Beef in Red Wine with Stilton and Rosemary Scones, page 27) or top with puff pastry and bake in a hot oven until the pastry is risen and crisp.

Serves 6 | Takes 15 minutes to make, 50 minutes to cook

1 tbsp olive oil
8 small shallots
3 carrots, diced
6 rashers smoked streaky bacon, sliced
600g minced venison
3 cloves garlic, sliced
2 tsp plain flour
350ml white wine
1 chicken stock cube
1–2 tbsp cranberry sauce
75g dried cranberries
200g cooked vacuum-packed chestnuts

Heat the oil in a pan and fry the shallots, carrots and bacon for 10 minutes until they have softened and the bacon is crisp. Add the garlic and venison and fry for 5 minutes until browned.

Sprinkle over the flour, stir well, then gradually add the wine and crumbled stock cube and enough boiling water to make a rich sauce, stirring until thickened. Add the cranberry sauce, dried cranberries and chestnuts and bring to the boil. Lower the heat, cover and simmer for 40 minutes until tender. Serve with plenty of mashed potatoes and a green vegetable.

Freeze for up to 3 months. Defrost in the fridge overnight and reheat thoroughly.

Marrow stuffed with venison and beef

This recipe comes from Mark Leatham, founder of Merchant Gourmet (they make lovely foodie ingredients) who is a passionate hunter-shooter-gatherer and who now farms rare breed White Park cattle in Dorset. His advice is to use boneless meat from the shoulder, neck and breast of the carcass and mix it with 30–40% of good fatty beef (usually brisket but other fatty cuts will do). Mark warns against using farmed venison as he believes there is simply no flavour to it; in his view you might as well use typically un-flavoursome beef. He asks his butcher to mix the diced meat up well and pass it through the mincer once.

Serves 4–6 | Takes 35 minutes to make, 40 minutes to cook

1 tbsp sunflower oil
1 onion, chopped
250g minced wild venison
250g minced beef
1 tbsp chopped fresh parsley
leaves from a few sprigs of thyme
1 tsp dried oregano
$\frac{1}{2}$ tsp dried chilli flakes
400g can chopped tomatoes
2 tbsp tomato purée
1 marrow (about 1.25kg)
100g Merchant Gourmet SunBlush® tomatoes, drained and chopped
1 tbsp olive oil
75g mature Cheddar cheese, grated
salt and freshly ground black pepper
Worcestershire sauce

Heat the oil in a large saucepan and fry the onions for 5 minutes until tender and beginning to brown, add the mince and fry, stirring, until browned and broken up. Add the herbs, chilli chopped tomatoes and tomato purée. Bring to the boil, then cover and simmer for 30 minutes.

Meanwhile, set the oven to 180°C/160°C fan/gas 4. Cut the marrow in half lengthways and scoop out the seeds in the centre. Brush with oil and a sprinkle of salt and black pepper and place on a baking tray in the oven. Cook for about 15 minutes until half cooked (this depends on the size but it should just feel a little tender).

When the mince is cooked add the coarsely chopped SunBlush® tomatoes to the mix. Spoon a generous amount of the cooked mince into the marrow shells, cover with foil and cook for another 15–20 minutes in the oven until the marrow is cooked. Remove it from the oven and cover it with Cheddar and roast until the cheese has melted and browned a little. Worcestershire sauce drizzled over is an optional extra!

The mince is suitable for freezing but the marrow won't freeze well as it is too watery. Freeze the mince for up to 1 month.

Chilli con carne

This is a staple dish in our household. I like to use chilli powder and paprika rather than chillies as the strength of chillies varies so much and paprika helps give it a more rounded flavour. Just one teaspoon of hot chilli powder gives a nice heat, but increase by another half teaspoon if you like it more fiery. However, if you have fresh chillies, use 1 finely chopped chilli instead of the chilli powder. You can also add 2 squares of plain chocolate at the end of cooking to make a glossier rich sauce.

Serves 4–6 | Takes 15 minutes to make, 40 minutes to cook

500g minced beef
1 onion, chopped
1 red pepper, deseeded and cut into strips
2 cloves garlic, crushed
1 tsp ground cumin
1 tsp hot chilli powder or 1 tbsp mild chilli powder
1 tsp paprika
1 tsp dried oregano
400g can chopped tomatoes
2 tbsp tomato purée
150ml full-bodied red wine or full-flavoured beef stock
400g can red kidney beans, drained
1 tbsp Worcestershire sauce (optional)
salt and freshly ground black pepper

Dry-fry the beef and onion in a medium pan for 10 minutes until the meat is browned and the onion softened. Add the red pepper, garlic, spices and oregano and fry for 2–3 minutes then stir in the chopped tomatoes and tomato purée. Pour over the red wine or beef stock, and the drained red kidney beans. Bring to the boil then season to taste using the Worcestershire sauce if liked. Reduce the heat and simmer for 30 minutes. Serve with boiled rice, tortilla chips (below), sour cream and coriander.

Freeze for up to 3 months. Defrost overnight and reheat thoroughly.

Tortilla crisps

Cut a flour tortilla into triangles, drizzle with olive oil and sprinkle with paprika before baking in an oven set to 200°C/180°fan/gas 6 for a couple of minutes until crisp.

AWT's venison chilli for a crowd

I've known Antony Worrall Thompson for many years, he's such a kind, intelligent and generous chef with a wonderful family. I can just imagine him throwing open his kitchen to friends and family to share this recipe with them.

Serves 12 | Takes 40 minutes to make, plus overnight soaking for the beans, 3 hours 40 minutes to cook

50g lard or 2 tablespoons olive oil
2kg coarsely minced venison
1kg onions, finely diced
3 cloves garlic, finely diced
3 sticks celery, chopped
3–4 chillies, finely diced
500g streaky bacon, diced into little cubes
2 x 400g cans chopped tomatoes
1 bay leaf
2 tbsp ground cumin
1 tbsp ground coriander
2 tbsp dried oregano
1½ tbsp paprika
1 tbsp fennel seed
1 tbsp cayenne pepper, to taste
1 tbsp unsweetened cocoa powder
1 tsp ground cinnamon
approximately 1 litre beef stock
2 tablespoons tomato purée
1 tbsp ground black pepper
500g red kidney beans, soaked overnight in cold water and drained
coriander leaves

Heat the lard or oil in a large ovenproof casserole and brown the venison, working in batches if necessary, and set aside.

In the casserole, fry the onion, garlic, celery and chillies in the fat until golden brown. Add the bacon, herbs and spices and fry until brown.

Return the meat to the pan and add all the other ingredients except the beans and coriander leaves. Bring to the boil then reduce the heat, cover and simmer for two hours. Add the beans, bring to the boil and be sure to boil rapidly for 10 minutes, stirring now and again, then lower the heat, cover and cook for a further 1½ hours or until the beans are cooked. Keep the beans covered with juices and add more stock if required. Stir in the coriander leaves just before serving.

Stuffed tomatoes

This makes a great supper, with just a simple green salad to accompany. If you have any filling left over, you can serve it alongside the tomatoes. This stuffing works just as well for hollowed-out aubergines and courgettes.

Serves 6 | Takes 25 minutes to make, 20 minutes to cook

50g long grain rice
6 large, firm beef or Dutch tomatoes
200g minced lamb
1/2 onion, finely diced
25g pecorino or Parmesan cheese, grated
1/2 tsp dried oregano
salt and freshly ground black pepper
100g sun-blush tomatoes, chopped
50g stoned black olives, chopped

Set the oven to 200°C/180°fan/gas 6.

Cook the rice in boiling, salted water for 12 minutes until tender and fluffy. Cut the tops off the tomatoes and, with a spoon, scoop out the seeds and core and set aside.

Dry-fry the lamb and onion in a large pan for 5 minutes until browned all over. Add the remaining ingredients together with the cooked rice and the tomato pulp and season with 1/2 teaspoon of salt and plenty of pepper. Simmer for 10 minutes. Taste and adjust the seasoning if necessary.

Pack the filling into the tomatoes and place in a roasting dish. Cover with foil and bake for 15–20 minutes until the tomatoes are tender.

Not suitable for freezing.

ROLL UP, ROLL UP'

Have you noticed that there's been a meatball revival? No longer the butt of jokes, meatballs now make for a popular great-value supper. I used to think life was too short to roll meatballs but now confess to being totally converted. By adding a few breadcrumbs and a sprinkle of herbs you can transform any kind of mince into a novel and rather wonderful meal. They can be shaped and stuffed with cheese and cooked in any number of rich and mouthwatering sauces. Meatballs are fun to make, fun to eat and deserve to be taken more seriously, please!

Asian-spiced patties with mango salsa

This is a great summer dish. Serve as an alternative to burgers.

**Serves 4 | Takes 20 minutes
to make, 8 minutes to cook**

500g lean minced beef
1 onion, grated
2 cloves garlic, crushed
2.5cm piece fresh root ginger,
    finely chopped
1 tbsp garam masala
salt and freshly ground black
    pepper
1–2 tbsp chopped fresh coriander

For the mango salsa
1 ripe mango, stoned and finely
    chopped
1 small red onion, finely chopped
1 red chilli, deseeded and finely
    chopped, optional
2 tbsp chopped fresh mint
1 tbsp chopped fresh coriander
grated zest and juice of1 lime

naan or torn Romaine lettuce
    leaves, to serve

**You will need 12 metal skewers,
    or 12 wooden skewers soaked in
    cold water for at least 10 minutes**

In a large, shallow bowl mix all the patty ingredients together. Using slightly damp hands to divide the mixture into 12 pieces and roll into small burger shapes. Cover and chill for 20 minutes.

Meanwhile, to make the salsa, mix all the ingredients together in a large bowl, cover and chill until ready to serve.

Preheat the grill or barbecue to hot.

Thread the patties onto skewers and grill or barbecue for 3–4 minutes on each side until cooked through. Serve with naan bread or Romaine lettuce leaves.

The salsa and patties can be made up to a day in advance, keep chilled in the fridge until ready to cook. Freeze the patties for up to 1 month. Defrost in the fridge before grilling or barbecueing.

BEEF

Angela Hartnett's meat balls with tomato sauce

Angela supplied recipes to a feature we used to run in *Delicious* magazine. I learnt such a lot of 'cheffy' tips from her. Her meatballs use milk and bread to make them nice and light. She also suggests adding a bit of Tabasco sauce if you want to spice them up. This great recipe is taken from her book, *Angela Hartnett's Cucina* (Ebury Press).

Serves 4 | Takes 45 minutes to make, 1 hour to cook

For the meatballs
6 tbsp milk
1 thick slice of stale white bread, crusts removed
500g good-quality minced beef
1 small onion, finely chopped
1 tbsp finely chopped fresh flat-leaf parsley
4 tbsp Parmesan cheese, freshly grated
1 egg, beaten
flour, for dusting
200ml olive oil, for frying
salt and freshly ground black pepper

For the tomato sauce
4 tbsp olive oil
1 onion, finely chopped
2 x 400g cans plum tomatoes
1 clove garlic, finely chopped
2 tsp tomato purée
pinch sugar
1 sprig fresh rosemary
olive oil, to drizzle

First, make the tomato sauce. Heat the olive oil in a pan over a medium heat. Add the onion and cook for 5 minutes or until soft and translucent.

Roughly squash the tomatoes with either your hands or a fork. Add them, and the juice from the cans, to the pan along with the garlic, tomato purée, sugar and rosemary. Lower the heat and simmer for 25–35 minutes or until the sauce is thick and jam-like in consistency. Remove the rosemary sprig and finish with a drizzle of extra virgin olive oil.

Put the milk in a bowl, soak the bread in it, then mash together with a fork. In another bowl mix together the beef, onion, parsley and Parmesan. Season well. Add the bread mixture to the beef, then mix in the beaten egg. Before you make the meatballs, check that the seasoning is right by frying and tasting a spoonful of it, adjusting the seasoning as necessary.

With floured hands, roll pieces of the mixture into balls about 5cm in diameter. Set aside.

In a wide shallow pan large enough to hold all the meatballs in one layer, heat the olive oil over a medium heat. Add the meatballs and cook until browned all over, turning very gently to prevent them breaking up. Remove from the pan and drain off the excess oil.

Return the meatballs to the pan and pour over the tomato sauce. Cover with baking parchment or foil, and cook gently over a low heat for 25 minutes. Serve with sautéed potatoes.

The sauce can be made in advance and stored in the fridge for up to 4 days, or freeze until ready for use. The meatballs can be stored in the refrigerator for up to 2 days.

Mozzarella meatballs and spaghetti with a roasted pepper sauce

These big meaty meatballs have a hidden surprise of melting cheese. They would also be nice made with lamb or pork mince too. Use a jar of pasta sauce if you want to make this dish even faster.

Serves 4–6 | Takes 30 minutes to make, 35 minutes to cook

For the meatballs
500g minced beef
50g fresh breadcrumbs
2 cloves garlic, crushed
1 tsp salt
$\frac{1}{2}$ tsp freshly ground black pepper
small handful fresh parsley, finely chopped
1 tsp dried oregano
75g Mozzarella cheese
3 tbsp rapeseed oil

For the sauce
1 small onion, diced
2 roasted red peppers (from a jar)
2 tbsp tomato purée
juice 1 orange
200ml beef stock
1 tbsp balsamic vinegar
50g stoned green olives, sliced
spaghetti, to serve

To make the meatballs, mix the minced beef with the breadcrumbs, garlic, seasoning, parsley and oregano. Mix well with damp hands and shape into 10–12 large meatballs about the size of a golf ball. Cut the Mozzarella into 10–12 chunks. Flatten each meatball and press a piece of cheese into the centre. Gather the meat around it and pinch to make sure it is sealed.

Heat the oil in a large shallow pan and fry the meatballs for about 10 minutes, turning occasionally. Remove from the pan and set aside.

To make the sauce, fry the onion in the pan juices until softened, add the peppers, tomato purée, orange juice, stock and vinegar. Bring to the boil, then using a hand blender, purée the sauce a little. Return the meatballs to the pan and simmer for 25 minutes until cooked through. Just before serving add the olives. Serve with spaghetti.

Freeze the meatballs in the sauce for up to 1 month. Defrost in the fridge before reheating thoroughly.

Mint and parsley meatballs in a lemon and coriander sauce

A jar of pasta sauce will suffice, but this sauce is so simple, takes no time at all and lifts the dish so nicely that you really should give it a try. It's especially good served with couscous.

Serves 4–6 | Takes 30 minutes to make, 40 minutes to cook

For the sauce
1 tsp coriander seeds
2 tbsp olive oil
1 onion, finely chopped
juice $\frac{1}{2}$ lemon
400g can chopped tomatoes
1 tbsp tomato purée
salt and freshly ground black pepper

For the meatballs
500g minced beef (or a mix of beef and lamb)
6 mint leaves, finely chopped
2 tbsp parsley finely chopped
1 tsp ground cumin
1 tsp salt
1 tsp freshly ground black pepper
2 tbsp sunflower oil

To make the sauce, dry-fry the coriander seeds in a small pan for 2–3 minutes then crush lightly with a pestle and mortar. Heat the oil in a medium shallow pan, add most of the onion, saving about 1 tablespoon for the meatballs. Fry until softened and beginning to brown. Add the lemon juice, crushed coriander, tomatoes and tomato purée, bring to the boil and then remove from the heat. Season to taste.

To make the meatballs, mix the minced beef with the mint, parsley, cumin and seasoning. Fry a little of the mixture to taste, and adjust seasoning if necessary. With damp hands, shape the mince into small golf-ball-sized balls. Chill if you have time.

Heat the oil in a large frying pan and fry the meatballs for 10 minutes, turning until browned. Add the sauce, bring to the boil then reduce the heat and simmer for 30 minutes.

Freeze the meatballs in the sauce for up to 1 month. Defrost in the fridge before reheating thoroughly.

Pork keftaides with halloumi and tzatziki

These are ideal hot or cold as a little starter or on a buffet table. The grated potato gives the meatballs a light texture and the flour makes them crisp and golden when fried.

Serves 6 | Takes 30 minutes to make, 30 minutes to cook

450g minced pork
$1/2$ onion, finely diced
2 cloves garlic, finely chopped
$1/2$ tsp salt and freshly ground
   black pepper
15g chopped fresh parsley
1 tsp dried oregano
1 potato (about 175g), peeled
2 tbsp flour, for dusting
4 tbsp vegetable oil, for frying

For the tzatziki
$1/2$ cucumber
1 clove garlic, crushed
150ml Greek yoghurt
15g fresh mint leaves, finely
   chopped
salt, freshly ground black pepper
squeeze lemon juice

1 tbsp vegetable oil, for frying
250g halloumi cheese, cut into
   1cm slices

Mix the pork, onion, garlic, $1/2$ teaspoon of salt, pepper and herbs together. Coarsely grate the potato into the mixture. Fry a little mixture in hot oil and taste, then adjust seasoning if necessary. Shape the mince into large marble-sized balls and drop onto a plate with the flour. Roll in the flour to coat. Chill while making the tzatziki salad.

Coarsely grate the cucumber and mix with the garlic, yoghurt and mint. Add a squeeze of lemon juice and season well. Chill.

Heat the oil until a small piece of the meatball sizzles as soon as it is added. Add the meatballs a few at a time and fry over a medium heat for 12–15 minutes, turning occasionally and lowering the heat if they get too brown, until golden and crisp on the outside but cooked and no longer pink in the centre. Keep warm in a hot oven while you cook the remainder.

Add a tablespoon of oil to a hot frying pan or griddle pan and fry the halloumi slices until just golden on both sides. Serve with the meatballs and the tzatziki.

The meatballs can be frozen for up to 3 months. Defrost in the fridge overnight before frying gently until reheated thoroughly.

Tana Ramsay's red pepper and apple meatballs with sweet and sour sauce

Tana very kindly gave me a copy of her book, *Tana Ramsay's Family Kitchen* (Harper Collins) after a food shoot at her house. It's full of the kind of recipes my family love. These meatballs are definitely a winner.

Serves 4–6 | Takes 25 minutes to make, 20 minutes to cook

For the meatballs
450g lean minced lamb
450g lean minced pork
1 red pepper, deseeded and finely
  chopped
1 small onion, finely chopped
3 Cox's apples, finely grated
2cm piece of fresh root ginger, grated
4 tsp chopped fresh coriander
1 egg white
flour, for dusting
2 tsp olive oil, for frying

For the sauce
2 tsp olive oil
1 red onion, finely chopped
4 baby leeks, chopped
1 courgette, sliced
450g cherry tomatoes, halved
salt and freshly ground black pepper
2 tsp brown sugar
2 tsp malt vinegar
6 fresh basil leaves, torn
300g basmati rice

Place the lamb and the pork mince into a large mixing bowl, and break it up a little. Add the finely chopped red pepper and onion, and then the grated apples, ginger and coriander. Add the egg white and mix together.

Shape the mixture into balls approximately 2cm in diameter and place on a tray lightly dusted with flour. Roll gently in the flour then place the tray in the fridge.

Meanwhile, make the sauce. In a medium frying pan heat up the olive oil and gently fry the onion until softened. Add the leeks and courgette and let them colour slightly, then add the halved tomatoes and let it all soften together. Check the seasoning, and add the brown sugar and malt vinegar. Let the sauce simmer gently. After about 20 minutes put the sauce in a liquidizer and whizz until smooth. Place back into the saucepan and set aside.

In a separate pan of water cook the rice.

Heat up the 2 teaspoons of olive oil for the meatballs. I usually use two medium-sized deep frying pans for this. Get the tray of meatballs out of the fridge and, when the oil is nice and hot, place the meatballs in over a moderate heat, turning to ensure they are cooking evenly. After about 10 minutes, ladle in the tomato sauce and allow this to heat thoroughly, until it is bubbling gently with the meatballs. Leave this to simmer for 15 minutes.

Drain and serve the rice, ladle on the balls and sauce. Garnish with basil and enjoy.

This dish can be frozen for up to 1 month. Defrost overnight in the fridge before reheating thoroughly. The meatballs and sauce can also be frozen separately.

Turkey meatballs with cranberry and red wine sauce

This is a great way to use up leftover cranberry sauce, but if you're like me, you'll have a jar of cranberry sauce in your storecupboard all year round so why wait until Christmas to try this? If serving with rice, I sometimes like to fold in a couple of handfuls of spinach.

Serves 4 | Takes 20 minutes to make, 30 minutes to cook

500g minced turkey
1 small onion, finely diced
2 cloves garlic, crushed
50g dried cranberries
50g pine nuts, toasted
$\frac{1}{2}$ tsp paprika
pinch mixed spice
pinch ground cinnamon
1 tbsp chopped fresh coriander
1 tbsp chopped fresh mint
1 tsp salt freshly ground black pepper
flour, for dusting
2 tbsp rapeseed oil
200ml red wine
2 tbsp cranberry sauce
1 tsp cornflour
toasted ciabatta or rice, to serve

Place the turkey, onion, garlic, cranberries, pine nuts, spices, herbs and 1 teaspoon of salt and freshly ground black pepper in a mixing bowl and mix with your hands until well blended. Fry just a little of the mixture in hot oil to test the taste. Adjust the seasoning if necessary. Roll into walnut-sized balls and dust in flour to prevent sticking.

Heat the oil in a frying pan and fry the meatballs for 10 minutes, turning gently once or twice until browned all over. Pour over the red wine and stir in the cranberry sauce. Bring to the boil, then reduce the heat and simmer for 15 minutes. Mix the cornflour with 1 tablespoon cold water and stir in. Cook for 1–2 minutes, stirring gently until the sauce is thickened. Serve with toasted ciabatta or rice.

Freeze the cooked meatballs in the sauce for up to 3 months. Defrost in the fridge overnight before reheating thoroughly.

Thai chicken balls with noodle soup

Fragrant and spicy, this is a great soup to serve when you are feeling cold. Add as little or as much chilli as you like. I like the soup clear, but the addition of coconut milk makes it rich and creamy too.

Serves 4 | Takes 20 minutes to make, 10 minutes to cook

For the meatballs
250g minced chicken or turkey
2 tsp red Thai curry paste
2 spring onions, chopped
1 tbsp chopped fresh coriander

For the soup
900ml good quality chicken stock
2 stalks lemongrass
3 cloves garlic, crushed
1–2 small red chillies depending on heat, finely sliced
125g rice noodles or 2 x 150g straight-to-wok cooked noodles
150g shiitake mushrooms, thinly sliced
1 red pepper, deseeded and sliced
150ml coconut milk (optional)
2–3 tbsp lime juice
15g roughly chopped fresh coriander, plus a little to garnish
1 tbsp Thai fish sauce (nam pla)
1 lime, cut into wedges, for serving

Place the mince, Thai curry paste, spring onions and coriander in a food processor and whizz until finely chopped. Turn out and shape the mixture into 16 small meatballs.

Heat the stock in a deep pan and turn heat to medium-high. Bruise the lemongrass by banging it with a rolling pin a couple of times then add it to the stock and boil for 5 minutes until fragrant. Add the garlic and chilli, then drop in the meatballs and bring to a rolling boil. Continue cooking for another 5 minutes.

Add the noodles, mushrooms, and pepper and continue to cook for 8–10 minutes, or until the noodles are tender and the meatballs are cooked. Turn down the heat to low and add the coconut milk, lime juice, coriander and fish sauce. Taste and season, adding more chillies and/or fish sauce if liked.

Serve in bowls with coriander sprinkled over and quarters of fresh lime on the side. Not suitable for freezing.

Frikadeller with turnip mash and red cabbage

These Scandinavian meatballs are very delicate, light and fluffy. It is essential to blend the mince to a fine paste in the food processor so that you can beat in the milk and egg. Frying them in butter gives them richness but do serve with well-flavoured accompaniments such as the braised red cabbage and turnip mash here.

Serves 6 | Takes 40 minutes to make, 20 minutes to cook

For the turnip mash
400g floury potatoes (such as King Edward or Maris Piper), chopped
200g white turnips, finely chopped
plenty of butter and milk, to mash
salt and freshly ground black pepper

For the red cabbage
1 small red cabbage, finely shredded
2 cooking apples, peeled, cored and chopped
1 tbsp brown sugar
1 tbsp red wine vinegar
25g butter

For the frikadeller
500g minced pork (or 250g minced veal 250g minced pork)
1 onion, roughly chopped
2 tbsp chopped fresh parsley
leaves from 1 sprig fresh thyme
pinch ground nutmeg or mace
3 tbsp plain flour
200ml milk
1 egg
1 tsp salt
$\frac{1}{2}$ tsp ground black pepper
75g butter
1 tbsp sunflower oil

First, make the turnip mash. Put the potatoes and turnips into a large pan of lightly salted water and cook for about 15–20 minutes, until tender. Drain and add plenty of butter and milk. Season with salt and pepper and mash until smooth and creamy.

Meanwhile, make the red cabbage. Into a pan, layer the red cabbage and the cooking apples and then add the brown sugar, red wine vinegar and the butter. Cover and cook over a low heat, for about 15 minutes, until tender.

Whilst the mash and cabbage are cooking, make the meatballs. Place the minced meat and onion in a food processor with the parsley and thyme, whizz until the mixture is finely minced. Turn into a bowl and add the nutmeg or mace seasoning and flour. Mix well then gradually add the milk a couple of spoonfuls at a time, beating with a wooden spoon to help aerate the mixture. Beat in the egg.

Heat the oil and butter in a frying pan and fry a little mixture for a couple of minutes until cooked, taste and adjust the seasoning in the remaining mixture if necessary.

Shape the mixture into oval meatballs by scooping out with 2 teaspoons dipped in water. Heat the butter and oil until foaming then add the meatballs a few at a time and fry until browned all over (keep warm in the oven while frying the remaining mixture). Serve with the red cabbage and turnip mash.

The meatballs can be frozen for up to 3 months. Defrost in the fridge overnight before frying gently for about 15 minutes or until reheated thoroughly.

Gushtaba

Meena Patak, co-founder of the Indian food brand, Pataks, created this recipe for me when I was editor of *Delicious* magazine several years ago. This spicy meatballs dish originates from Hyderabad and has a divine creamy yoghurt sauce.

Serves 4 | Takes 25–30 minutes to make, 25–30 minutes to cook

500g finely minced lamb
1 tsp ground paprika
1/4 tsp chilli powder
1 tsp fennel seeds, crushed
1/2 tsp ground coriander
1 tsp freshly ground black pepper
1/4 tsp ground cardamom
2cm piece fresh ginger, finely grated
120g natural yoghurt
plain flour, for dusting
1 tbsp ghee or vegetable oil
1 tbsp Pataks Rogan Josh Curry Paste
200ml whipping cream
large pinch unrefined sugar
salt
1 tsp garam masala

Put the mince into a large bowl. Add the paprika, chilli powder, fennel seeds, coriander, pepper, cardamom, and ginger. Add 1 tablespoon yoghurt and use your hands to mix everything together. Shape into 16–18 balls, using a little flour to prevent sticking.

Heat the ghee or oil in a frying pan and fry the meatballs in batches if necessary for 10–15 minutes until cooked. Drain on kitchen paper.

Add the curry paste to the pan and cook for 1 minute. Stir in the cream, sugar and a little salt. Return the meatballs to the pan and heat through. Stir in the remaining yoghurt and the garam masala. Serve in bowls with chapattis or basmati rice.

The meatballs can be frozen – cooked or uncooked – for up to 1 month. Defrost overnight in the fridge before frying in hot oil until thoroughly cooked or reheated. Then make the sauce and heat through with the meatballs.

HUMBLE PIES

There's always a noticeable murmur of appreciation when a comforting homemade pie is served. Quick-to-cook mince and readymade pastry make the job much easier (though homemade pastry will win you even more applause, of course). Try the ever-so-easy savoury mince pies to serve for a drinks party, the classic pasties for a filling handheld lunch, or posh up your picnics and plump for the delectably rich and nutty Huntsman's pies.

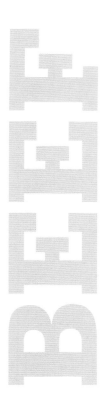

Beef, Guinness and oyster mushroom pie

Everyone loves a meat pie. As minced beef is so quick to cook you may find it easier and even quicker to cook a circle of puff pastry separately in the oven then cut into wedges and serve on top of the mince, rather than cooking a whole pie.

Serves 4 | Takes 20 minutes to make, 30 minutes to cook

500g minced beef
1 onion, cut into 8 wedges
2 carrots, diced
1 tbsp plain flour
2 tbsp tomato purée
400ml can Guinness
100ml strong beef stock
1 tbsp brown sugar
2 tsp Dijon mustard
1 bay leaf
250g oyster mushrooms
375g ready-rolled puff pastry
1 egg yolk, to glaze

In a large pan, dry-fry the minced beef and onions for 5 minutes or until browned. Add the carrots along with the flour and tomato purée. Stir well and gradually add the Guinness, stock, sugar, mustard and bay leaf. Simmer for 15 minutes until the meat is tender and the sauce has thickened. Roughly break up the mushrooms and stir into the mince. Leave to cool before making the pie.

Set the oven to 200°C/180°C fan/gas 6.

Pour the meat into a 1-litre pie dish. Unroll the pastry and cut to the size of the dish. Cut the trimmings into strips and place these around the dampened edge of the dish. Dampen with a little water then place the pastry over the top and press down well to seal. Brush the egg yolk over the pastry. Bake in the oven for 30 minutes until golden and risen.

Freeze for up to 3 months. Defrost in the fridge overnight before reheating thoroughly.

Turkish pastries

These make a tasty nibble for canapé parties or as part of a meze table.

Makes 12 | Takes 30 minutes to
make, 20 minutes to cook

1 tbsp olive oil
2 onions, finely chopped
300g minced chicken or turkey
1 tbsp pine nuts
1 tbsp raisins
$\frac{1}{2}$ tsp ground allspice
pinch nutmeg, grated
1 tbsp chopped fresh parsley
zest and juice $\frac{1}{2}$ lemon
100g feta cheese, crumbled
500g ready-rolled puff pastry

Put the olive oil into a medium-sized saucepan and fry the onions until tender then add the chicken and fry, stirring until browned. Add the nuts, raisins, allspice, nutmeg and parsley, lemon zest and juice. Season with plenty of salt and black pepper and cook for 2–3 minutes until most of the liquid has evaporated. Add the crumbled feta cheese.

Set the oven to 200°C/180°C fan/gas 6. Unroll the pastry and cut into 12–16 8cm circles using a pastry cutter. Brush the edges of the pastry circles with water then pile a good teaspoonful of mixture in the centre of each one. Fold up 3 sides of each circle, pinching the folds to make a triangular shape with the centre still open to reveal the filling.

Place on a baking tray and bake for 20 minutes until golden brown. Serve hot or cold.

Not suitable for freezing.

Cornish pasties

I grew up in Devon and have always loved pasties. Mum always made a stash of them to take on a picnic and would wrap the pasties in a container with a blanket around to keep them warm in the back of our Mini Cooper until we arrived at our picnic destination. I often make them now for picnics with my children too. True Cornish pasties are made with chuck steak, potato and swede but this is a more economical recipe. To me, one of the essential tastes of a pasty is lots of pepper and plenty of swede. I've made proper pasty pastry which uses strong flour to make them crisp and robust, but you can, of course, use readymade shortcrust for speed. Traditionally, the pasties were folded onto their side and the pastry crimped and rolled to make a thick 'handle' for Cornish tin miners to hold when carrying their lunch, but in Devon we fold both sides of the pastry up over the filling and crimp the edge.

Makes 8 pasties | Takes 30–40 minutes to make, 50–60 minutes to cook

650g minced beef
1 onion, finely diced
600g potatoes, finely diced
1 small swede (about 400g), finely diced
150ml beef stock
½ tsp salt
2–3 tsp freshly ground back pepper

For the pastry
125g block or hard margarine
500g strong white flour
125g lard
a little beaten egg or milk, to glaze

First of all, place the margarine for the pastry in the freezer to chill while making the filling. Dry-fry the minced beef and onion in a medium pan for 5 minutes until browned all over. Add the potato and swede to the mince mixture with the stock, bring to the boil then reduce the heat and simmer for 5 minutes. Taste and season well with the salt and pepper. Allow to cool before making the pasties.

Make the pastry. Place the flour in a bowl and rub in the lard. Grate the frozen margarine on the coarse side of a grater and add to the flour. Stir well, then add 12–14 tablespoons of cold water, mixing with a knife until well mixed. Knead the mixture well, wrap in clingfilm and leave to rest for 30 minutes before using (it is even better chilled overnight).

Set the oven to 180°C/fan 160°C/gas 4.

Divide the pastry into 8 balls. Roll out each one to a 12cm circle. Place about an eighth of the mixture into the centre of each pastry circle. Brush one half of the edge of pastry with water then fold over the filling onto the other side and press down well to seal in the filling. Crimp the edge and repeat with the remaining pasties. Place on a baking tray.

Brush the pasties with a little beaten egg or milk to glaze, then bake them for 50–60 minutes, until golden brown. Serve hot or cold.

These can be frozen for up to 3 months. Defrost overnight before thoroughly reheating in an oven set to 180°C/fan 160°C/gas 4.

Thanksgiving turkey turnovers

I suppose I could call these Christmas pasties too, but the addition of sweet potato mash gives them an American twist. You could, of course, use cold leftover turkey and Christmas stuffing too to make these tasty snacks, ideal for a light supper or lunch.

Makes 6 pasties | Takes 20 minutes to make, 20–25 minutes to cook

1 sweet potato
1 tbsp sunflower oil
1 small onion, finely diced
2 rashers bacon
250g minced turkey
pinch dried chilli powder
1 sage leaf, finely chopped
1 tbsp cranberry sauce, plus extra to serve
500g ready-rolled puff pastry (or 1 pack Jus Rol Individual Puff Pastry Rounds)

Set the oven to 220°C/200°C fan/gas 7.

Pierce the sweet potato with a knife and microwave on high for 3–4 minutes until tender (or bake in the preheated oven for 20–30 minutes). Cut in half and scoop out the flesh.

Heat the oil in a medium saucepan and fry the onion and bacon for 5 minutes until softened. Add the minced turkey, a little pinch of dried chilli powder and the sage and fry until the meat is browned. Cover and cook over a low heat for 10 minutes. Stir in the cranberry sauce and sweet potato. Remove from the pan and place in a bowl to cool a little.

Cut the puff pastry into six 17cm circles. Place a spoonful of the cooled mixture onto one half of each pastry circle. Dampen the edge with water and fold over. Press well to seal.

Place on a baking tray and bake for 20–25 minutes until golden, risen and puffy. Serve warm with extra cranberry sauce.

Freeze for up to 3 months. Bake from frozen in an oven set to 220°C/200°C fan/gas 7 for 20 minutes until thoroughly hot.

Pirozhki

Pirozhki means 'little pies', and this Russian dumpling recipe is adapted from Silvena Rowe's *Feasts* book (Mitchell Beazley) a delicious collection of recipes from Central and Eastern Europe. I love the sour cream pastry and use it for lots of other pies too. You can also use minced beef in the filling – traditionally mixed with chopped hard boiled eggs too.

Serves 6 | Takes 45 minutes to make plus chilling time, 25 minutes to cook

For the pastry
200g plain flour, plus extra
    for dusting
½ tsp salt
½ tsp baking powder
100g butter, chilled
2 large egg yolks
125ml sour cream

For the filling
2 tbsp vegetable oil
1 onion, finely chopped
200g minced turkey or chicken
2 tbsp chopped fresh parsley
1 tbsp chopped fresh dill
3 tbsp sour cream
2 large egg yolks, beaten

To make the pastry, place the flour, salt and baking powder into a large mixing bowl. Add the butter, cut into pieces, and rub into the flour using your fingertips, until the mixture looks like breadcrumbs. Add the egg yolks and sour cream and bring the dough together to make a soft elastic dough. Wrap in clingfilm and chill for 1 hour.

Meanwhile make the filling. Heat the oil in a frying pan and fry the onion for 5 minutes until soft and transparent. Add the mince and fry until browned. Cook for 10 minutes over a low heat, then place in a bowl to cool.

When ready to make the pastries, add the herbs and sour cream to the chicken mixture.

Set the oven to 190°C/170°C fan/gas 5. Dust the work surface with a little flour and roll out half the dough until it is 3–4mm thick. Using a 8cm pastry cutter, cut out as many circles as you can. Brush the edges of the pastry with a little egg yolk, and place a spoonful of mixture into the centre. Fold over to make half moon shapes and press edges together. Repeat with the rest of the filling and pastry. Place the pirozhki on a baking sheet, brush the tops with the beaten egg yolk and bake for 25 minutes.

Not suitable for freezing.

Pork and leek pies

These deliciously simple pork pies are good to eat either hot or cold. Use 600g readymade pastry if you prefer, but there's nothing nicer than homemade!

Makes 8 pies | Takes 45 minutes to make, 20 minutes to cook

500g minced pork
3 rashers smoked streaky bacon or pancetta
3 shallots finely diced
1 leek, thinly sliced and rinsed
2 sage leaves, finely chopped
4 tbsp crème fraîche
salt and freshly ground black pepper

For the pastry
400g plain flour
100g lard
100g butter or margarine
flour, for dusting

Dry-fry the minced pork with the bacon, shallots, leeks and sage for about 5 minutes until browned and the shallots and leeks are beginning to soften. Season with plenty of salt and black pepper to taste. Cover, reduce the heat and simmer for 10 minutes. Allow to cool while making the pastry.

Place the flour in a bowl and add the lard and butter. Cut the fat into small pieces then rub the fat into the flour between your fingertips until it resembles fine breadcrumbs. Add 6–8 tablespoons cold water and mix in until the mixture forms a dough. Wrap in clingfilm and chill in the fridge for 30 minutes if you have time.

Set the oven to 220°C/200°C fan/gas7.

Turn the pastry out onto a well floured board and cut out eight 12cm circles using a small bowl or saucer as a guide. Place each circle of pastry inside a deep muffin tin and press the pastry against the sides, easing out the pleats of pastry but leaving the top edge a bit uneven.

Stir the crème fraîche into the pork mixture then divide between the pastry cases. Re-roll the pastry trimmings and cut out eight 7cm pastry circles. Dampen the edges with a little water and turn dampened side down on top of the pies. Press the edges of the pastry together. Bake for 20 minutes until golden brown and crisp. Serve hot or cold.

Not suitable for freezing.

Picnic egg pie

This recipe dates back to the thrifty '50s and was originally made without pastry, steamed in a muslin cloth for 3 hours then rolled in breadcrumbs, but I've wrapped it in pastry to make it look and taste more appealing. It is perfect to slice on a picnic when everyone is starving, or makes a great cold lunch with salad. You could also make individual pies. Buy lean mince and good quality sausages for the best results or it will be too fatty. If you make this without the pastry, put the meat into a 1kg loaf tin and bake in an oven set to 190°C/170°C fan/gas 5. Cook for 45–60 minutes until it's firm to the touch and the juices run clear when the centre is pierced with a knife. When cold, it will slice thinly for sandwiches.

Serves 6–8 | Takes 20 minutes to make, 45 minutes to cook

3 eggs
100g back bacon
1 small onion
50g fresh bread
small handful fresh parsley
250g minced beef
250g good quality pork sausagemeat
1 tsp salt
1 tsp freshly ground black pepper
1 tsp English mustard powder
375g pack chilled shortcrust pastry
flour, for dusting

Boil the eggs for 8 minutes, then cool and remove the shells.

Meanwhile, remove the rind from the bacon and place in a food processor with the onion, bread and parsley. Whizz until finely chopped. Turn into a mixing bowl and add the beef, sausagemeat, seasoning and mustard powder. Mix really well with your hands until combined.

Set the oven to 220°C/200°C fan/gas 7.

Dust a work surface with flour and roll out the pastry to a rectangle about 30 x 25cm. Place half the meat mixture down the centre leaving 5cm all around to fold over. Lay the eggs down the centre of the pastry and place the remaining meat mixture on top ensuring the eggs are enclosed. Using a pastry brush or your fingers, dampen the edges of the pastry and fold the pastry up and over the meat like a parcel, folding up the ends. Carefully lift onto a baking tray and turn upside down so the fold is underneath. Pat into a neat shape and bake in the oven for 45 minutes. Serve at room temperature or cold.

Not suitable for freezing.

BEEF

Simple samosas

First of all, I must confess that these are not the real thing! Much as I love authentic samosas they are tricky to make and high in fat. This is my cheat's lower-fat version. Filo pastry makes a crisp wrapper for them, but it can be even quicker if you use Jus Rol Individual pastry rounds – simply add the filling, fold the pastry over and bake (you'll only need half the filling listed here per pack of pastry circles). This curry filling is also delicious served with rice, so why not turn it into two meals: curry tonight, samosas a day or two later!

Makes about 40 small samosas | Takes 40 minutes plus cooling to make, 12 minutes to cook

**500g minced beef
1 small onion, diced
2 tbsp curry paste such as
   Rogan Josh or balti
1 medium potato, cut into
   1cm dice
100g frozen peas
3–4 tbsp mango chutney
200g pack filo pastry
4 tbsp vegetable oil
extra mango chutney, to serve**

Dry-fry the mince and onion in a medium pan until browned all over. Add the curry paste and cook for 2–3 minutes then add 200ml of boiling water and the potato. Simmer gently for about 15 minutes until the mince and potatoes are tender.

Add the frozen peas and enough mango chutney to make the mixture moist but not wet. Allow the mixture to cool before wrapping in pastry.

Set oven to 220°C/200°C fan/gas 6.

Cut the filo pastry into 9cm x 30cm rectangles. Keep the pastry covered with a damp tea towel to prevent it from drying out. Brush one strip of pastry with oil. Place a spoonful of the mince mixture on the top corner of the pastry and fold the pastry over to make a triangle, flip the triangle over and keep rolling it in a triangle shape until the strip of pastry is used up and you have completely sealed the filling inside. Brush with a little more oil and place on a baking tray. Repeat with the pastry and mince until all the mixture is used. Bake for 12 minutes until golden brown and crisp. Serve with more mango chutney if liked.

Freeze cooked or uncooked for up to 1 month. Cook from frozen in an oven set to 200°C/180°C fan/ gas 6. for 15–20 minutes.

Moroccan-spiced pie with harissa yoghurt dressing

This is an unusual but delicious supper dish which would be ideal for a casual supper with friends, the harissa dressing really completes the meal.

Serves 6–8 | Takes 30 minutes to make, 30 minutes to cook

**500g minced lamb
1 clove garlic, crushed
1cm piece fresh root ginger, grated
$\frac{1}{2}$ tsp ground cumin
$\frac{1}{2}$ tsp ground coriander
$\frac{1}{2}$ tsp salt
4 medium carrots, grated
2 raw beetroots, grated
75g dried cranberries
100g pine nuts
25g butter
2 tbsp olive oil
200g filo pastry
freshly ground black pepper**

**For the harissa yoghurt
2–3 tsp harissa paste
200ml Greek yoghurt
2–3 tbsp milk
pinch paprika, to garnish**

Dry-fry the mince in a medium pan until browned all over. Add the garlic, ginger, spices and seasoning and fry for 2–3 minutes then add the carrots, beetroot, cranberries and most of the pine nuts, reserving a tablespoonful for decoration. Reduce the heat and simmer the mixture for 10–15 minutes, then allow to cool.

Set the oven at 220°C/200°C fan/gas 6.

Melt the butter and oil together in a small pan. Brush a 28cm round loose-bottomed fluted flan tin with the oil and butter, then lay one sheet of pastry in the base allowing a little to hang over the edges. Brush lightly with oil and butter then continue to layer up 8 sheets of pastry at alternate angles so that the whole base is covered and there is plenty hanging over the edges all around. Make sure you oil and butter each layer. Pile the cooled mince mixture into the tin and then bring the pastry up over the filling, scrunching the pastry on top. Add 5 or 6 more sheets of pastry scrunched up on top and drizzle with the remaining oil and butter.

Bake for 20 minutes then sprinkle with the remaining pine nuts and continue to bake for another 5–10 minutes until golden and crisp.

Mix the harissa paste with the yoghurt and milk and sprinkle with a little paprika. Slice and serve the pie hot.

Not suitable for freezing.

Savoury mince pies

Serve these little lamb and cranberry mince pies at a Christmas drinks party; they make a nice change from sweet mince pies. They are best served warm from the oven, but are good cold too.

Makes approximately 18 pies | Takes 30 minutes to make, 15 minutes to cook

250g minced lamb
1 red onion
3 sprigs fresh rosemary
pinch grated nutmeg
1 tbsp Worcestershire sauce
1 tbsp cranberry sauce
500g shortcrust pastry
1 egg, beaten
sea salt and freshly ground black
  pepper
flour, for dusting

Dry-fry the minced lamb and onion for 5 minutes until browned and the onion is beginning to soften. Chop a few needles of rosemary from just one sprig, and add to the pan. Reduce the heat and continue to cook for another 10 minutes. Add the nutmeg, Worcestershire sauce and cranberry sauce, season to taste and stir well. Allow to cool while rolling out the pastry.

Set the oven to 200°C/180°C fan/gas 6.

Dust a work surface with a little flour and roll out the pastry thinly to the thickness of a 2p piece. Using a plain pastry cutter, cut 18x7.5cm and 18x6.5cm circles, re-rolling the pastry if necessary. Place the larger circles in the base of bun or tartlet tins and add a spoonful of the lamb mixture to each, making sure there is plenty of mixture inside. Dampen the edge of the smaller pastry circles with a little water and place them on top of the mince, water side down. Press well with a fork to seal the edges.

Brush the beaten egg over the pies then sprinkle with salt and black pepper. Finally, poke a sprig of rosemary leaves into the centre of each one and bake for 15 minutes until golden brown. Allow them to cool a little before serving.

Freeze for up to 3 months. Defrost before reheating thoroughly.

LAMB

North African-style lamb and date filo purses

These are tasty little parcels to serve as part of a meze table – lots of little dishes to share, or make 8 larger pies to serve as a light lunch with a salad.

Makes 20 small purses |
Takes 40 minutes to make,
15 minutes to cook

500g minced lamb
1/2 onion, finely diced
1 clove garlic
1 sprig thyme
1/4 tsp paprika
1/4 tsp ground cumin
good pinch dried chilli flakes
1/4 tsp ground ginger
1 tsp salt
1 tsp black pepper
75g dates, roughly chopped
25g flaked almonds
juice of 1/2 lime
2 tbsp Greek yoghurt
200g filo pastry
1 tbsp olive oil
25g butter

Dry-fry the minced lamb and onion in a medium pan for 10 minutes until the meat has browned and the onion is tender. Add the garlic, thyme, spices and seasoning then add the dates, cook for 2–3 minutes then place in a bowl to cool. Fry the almonds in the pan (there's no need to clean the pan) and add to the mince with the lime juice and yoghurt.

Set the oven to 200°C/180°C fan/gas 6.

Unroll the filo pastry and cut into 8cm squares. Heat the oil and butter together until the butter just melts. Remove from the heat. Brush each square of filo very lightly with the melted butter and oil and layer 3 sheets together. Place a spoonful of mixture into the centre of each stack of pastry and fold up the 4 corners of the pastry, pinching them in the centre to make a scrunched parcel. Place on a baking sheet. Repeat with the remaining pastry and filling. Bake for 12–15 minutes until golden brown and cooked through. Serve hot or warm with salad.

Freeze cooked or uncooked for up to 3 months. Cook from frozen in a hot oven until thoroughly reheated.

Spring lamb, mint and apricot pot pies

These little pies are ideal for a spring lunch or supper, served hot from the oven.

Makes 4 individual pies |
Takes 25 minutes to prepare,
30 minutes to cook

500g minced lamb
1 red onion
2 tbsp tomato purée
150g ready-to-eat dried apricots, chopped
2–3 tsp mint sauce
1 tbsp Worcestershire sauce
2 tsp flour
200g frozen broad beans
1 egg, beaten
375g ready-made puff pastry
salt and freshly ground black pepper

Dry-fry the minced lamb and onion in a medium pan until the meat has browned and the onion is becoming tender. Add the tomato purée, apricots, mint sauce and Worcestershire sauce. Sprinkle with flour and stir for 1 minute then gradually pour on 150ml of water, stirring until thickened. Bring to the boil then simmer for 15–20 minutes. Season to taste and add more mint sauce, if liked. Stir in the broad beans, remove from heat and divide the mixture between 4 individual 18cm pie dishes and chill.

Set the oven to 200°C/180°C fan/gas 6.

Cut the pastry into 4 equal pieces and roll out on a lightly floured work surface to circles or squares large enough to drape over the top of the pie dishes. Brush the rim of the dish with beaten egg then place pastry over the top allowing it to drape over the sides. Make a slit in the centre of each pie for the steam to escape. I like to leave them untrimmed, but you may prefer to trim the pastry around the edge of the dish. Press the pastry well onto the rim and bake for 15–18 minutes until risen and golden brown.

Not suitable for freezing (the broad beans will become too tough).

Huntsman pies with walnut pastry

These great little posh pies are ideal to take on picnics or to serve for a summer party. They are quite filling so half a pie might be sufficient for some! I love the nutty pastry but you can of course use plain shortcrust.

Makes 6 pies | Takes 40 minutes to make, 30 minutes to cook

For the walnut pastry
50g lard
75g butter
75g walnuts, shelled
250g plain flour
flour, for dusting

For the filling
250g good quality pork sausages
500g minced game
1/2 onion, finely diced
2 tbsp chopped fresh parsley
5 juniper berries crushed
pinch grated nutmeg
grated zest 1/2 lemon
1 tsp salt
1 tsp freshly ground black pepper
flour, for dusting

You will need six 10 x 3cm deep fluted flan tins (I use Alan Silverwood tins – available from stockists such as John Lewis – that have really deep flutes).

To make the pastry, dice the lard and butter and place in a food processor with the walnuts and flour. Whizz until the mixture forms fine breadcrumbs. Add 3 tablespoons of cold water and whizz for a second or two more. Turn out onto a lightly floured work surface and bring the mixture into a smooth ball. Wrap in clingfilm and chill while making the filling.

Slip the skin off the sausages and place in a mixing bowl with the game mince, onion and parsley. Crush the juniper berries in a pestle and mortar, and add to the mince with the nutmeg, the lemon zest and salt and pepper. Mix well.

Set the oven to 220°C/200°C fan/gas 7.

Dust a worksurface lightly with flour. Roll out two thirds of the pastry and cut into 6 circles, 12cm in diameter, and use to line each flan tin. Divide the mince mixture between the flan cases piling it up a little in the centre. Dampen the edge of the pastry with a little water. Roll out the remaining pastry and cut out 6 further circles, 11cm in diameter, and place over the mince pressing down well at the edges to seal. Using the point of a knife, cut a cross in the top of each pie then place in the oven and bake for 30 minutes until golden. These can be served hot but are also really good served cold with some fruity chutney.

Not suitable for freezing.

PASSION FOR PASTA

Mince and pasta are perfect partners. Beyond family favourites such as spaghetti Bolognese and lasagne lie a whole host of wonderful combinations. From the simple wonders of Giancarlo Caldesi's ragu to comforting pasta bakes, nice gnocchi suppers and a speedy pappardelle dish too.

Red pesto Bolognese

This has become one of my favourite cheat recipes. A jar of red pesto added to mince makes a rich and delicious meal – great for family or for friends. Serve with everyday pasta shapes or fresh egg pasta to impress.

Serves 4 | Takes 25 minutes to make, 30 minutes to cook

500g minced lamb
1 onion, finely chopped
2 cloves garlic, crushed
2 red peppers, deseeded and finely sliced
190g jar red pesto
400g can chopped tomatoes
150g dried pasta shapes
grated Parmesan cheese, to serve (optional)

Dry-fry the mince with the onion until the onion has softened and the mince has browned. Add the garlic and fry for 1–2 minutes. Add the peppers, pesto and tomatoes and simmer for 20 minutes, stirring occasionally.

Meanwhile, cook the pasta in boiling water according to the pack instructions. Drain and stir into the meat sauce. Serve sprinkled with Parmesan, if liked.

Freeze for up to 3 months. Defrost overnight in the fridge and reheat thoroughly.

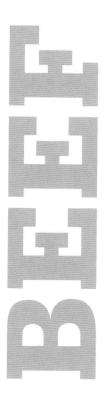

Lasagne

I couldn't do a mince book without lasagne, but there are so many variations that it was hard to choose which to do. As I want you to use this recipe as often as possible, I decided to give you the basic, everyday recipe that your family will ask for again and again. If you want to posh it up, you can use a mince mix that is half beef, half pork. You can also add chopped chicken livers or chopped pancetta, and you can layer up the lasagne sheets with slices of Mozzarella too or make the Béchamel richer by adding double cream. This is my family's favourite and I hope you enjoy it too.

Serves 6 | Takes 40 minutes to make, 30 minutes to cook

500g minced beef
1 onion, coarsely grated
1 carrot, finely diced
2 cloves garlic, crushed
1 tsp dried oregano
400g can tomatoes
2 tbsp tomato purée
100ml full-bodied red wine (or beef stock)
salt and freshly ground black pepper
250g pack fresh lasagne sheets

For the Béchamel
50g butter
50g plain flour
600ml full-fat milk
50g Parmesan, grated
grating of fresh nutmeg (optional)

Dry-fry the mince in a large saucepan with the onion and carrot until the meat is browned and the onion has begun to soften. Add the garlic and oregano and fry for 1–2 minutes, then pour over the tomatoes, tomato purée and red wine or stock. Stir well and bring to the boil, season to taste and simmer for 20 minutes.

Meanwhile, make the béchamel sauce. Melt the butter in a medium saucepan and add the flour. Stir well and cook for 1 minute until thickened. Gradually pour on the milk, stirring all the time and cooking after every addition until smooth and thick. Season with plenty of salt and pepper then stir in most of the Parmesan cheese. Grate in a little nutmeg, if liked.

Soak the lasagne sheets in boiling water or cook as directed on the pack. Set the oven to 180°C/160°C fan/gas 4.

Layer 2 sheets of lasagne in the base of a 1.5-litre shallow baking dish, top with a layer of mince, add another layer of lasagne sheets, a thin layer of Béchamel sauce and the remaining mince. Top with the two of lasagne sheets and spread with the remaining Béchamel sauce. Sprinkle with the remaining Parmesan cheese. Bake in the hot oven for 25–30 minutes until golden and bubbling.

Freeze for up to 3 months. Defrost overnight in the fridge and reheat thoroughly.

Pork and Parmesan cannelloni

If you like making lasagne, try this instead. I think this is actually quicker than lasagne as there's no white sauce to make. You simply roll up the meat mixture in lasagne sheets and top with the tomato sauce and cheese. A jar of tomato sauce makes it even quicker, of course. This recipe works every bit as well with beef, lamb or chicken mince. Chopped mushrooms, courgettes or spinach all make for perfect additions to the meat mixture too.

Serves 4 | Takes 30 minutes to make, 30 minutes to cook

For the meat filling and pasta
1 tbsp olive oil
400g minced pork
1 onion, roughly chopped
1 clove garlic, crushed
3 tbsp tomato purée
60g breadcrumbs
6 sheets (approximately 250g) quick-cook, fresh lasagne sheets
1 tsp dried oregano
1 egg
50g Parmesan cheese, grated
½ tsp salt
freshly ground black pepper

For the tomato sauce
1 tbsp olive oil
1 onion, finely chopped
1 clove garlic, crushed
1 red pepper, deseeded and finely chopped
600ml passata
1 tsp dried oregano
2 tsp sugar
1 tbsp balsamic vinegar

For the topping
100ml crème fraîche
150g Mozzarella cheese, sliced
50g Parmesan cheese, grated

Heat the oil in a medium saucepan and fry the mince, onion and garlic for 10 minutes until tender and until browned all over. Add the tomato purée and breadcrumbs and leave to cool while making the sauce. Soak the lasagne sheets in boiling water for 5 minutes or as directed on the pack, then drain.

Set the oven at 200°C/180°C fan/gas 6.

To make the tomato sauce, heat the oil in a medium pan and fry the onion, garlic and red pepper for 5 minutes until softened. Pour on the passata and add the oregano, sugar and vinegar. Bring to the boil and simmer for 5 minutes.

To assemble, mix the egg and Parmesan into the meat mixture with the salt and pepper and mix well. Divide the mixture into six portions and spoon one portion along the short end of a piece of lasagne. Roll it up and place into a large baking dish. Repeat with the remaining meat filling and lasagne sheets, placing into the baking dish and allowing a little space in between each one. Pour over the tomato sauce. Spread crème fraîche over the top, then arrange the Mozzarella on top and sprinkle with Parmesan. Bake in the oven for 30 minutes. Serve with a green salad.

Freeze for up to 3 months. Defrost overnight in the fridge and reheat thoroughly.

Meatball pasta bake

This is a comforting dish to serve to the family and can be made in advance ready to reheat the next day.

Serves 4 | Takes 40 minutes to make, 20 minutes to cook

300g penne pasta
500g minced beef
1 egg
1 tsp dried oregano
75g fresh breadcrumbs
1 tbsp olive oil
2 roasted red peppers (from a jar will do), chopped
420g jar tomato pasta sauce
150ml beef stock or red wine
50g fresh breadcrumbs
100g grated Mozzarella cheese
1 tbsp chopped fresh thyme

Set the oven to 180°C/160°C fan/gas 4.

Cook the pasta in boiling salted water for 10 minutes until just tender but still with a little bite as it will continue cooking later. Mix together the beef, egg, oregano, just 25g of the breadcrumbs and season well. Mix well and shape into about 20 meatballs.

Heat the oil in a large frying pan and fry the meatballs for about 10 minutes turning occasionally until browned. Add the red pepper, pasta sauce and 150ml of beef stock or red wine. Bring to the boil. Stir the drained pasta into the meatballs and pour into a 1.5 litre baking dish. Sprinkle with the breadcrumbs, Mozzarella and thyme and bake for 20 minutes until golden and bubbling.

Both the meatballs and the sauce can be made in advance and chilled in the fridge until ready to assemble and cook. Or the whole dish can be made and frozen for up to 3 months. Defrost overnight in the fridge before reheating thoroughly.

Cypriot pork pasta bake

A lovely rich creamy dish with a light taste of lemon and wine. If you don't have wine, use cider instead.

Serves 4 | Takes 30 minutes to make, 30 minutes to cook

500g minced pork
1 onion, finely diced
$\frac{1}{2}$ tsp salt
1 tbsp fresh, chopped parsley
grated zest $\frac{1}{2}$ lemon
pinch ground cinnamon
150ml dry white wine
250g rigatoni or large macaroni
freshly ground black pepper

For the sauce
50g butter
50g plain flour
450ml milk
100g haloumi cheese, finely chopped
salt and freshly ground black pepper

Fry the mince and onion in a large pan for about 10 minutes until the onion has softened and the meat has browned. Add the salt, pepper, parsley, lemon zest and cinnamon. Pour over the wine and bring to the boil. Cover and simmer for 15 minutes. Meanwhile, boil the rigatoni for 10 minutes until almost cooked but still with a good bite as it will continue cooking in the oven later.

Set the oven to 180°C/160°C fan/gas 4.

To make the sauce, melt the butter in a small pan and add the flour. Cook for 1 minute then gradually stir in the milk, beating well all the time until the sauce is smooth and thickened. Cook for 1 minute, then add the haloumi to the sauce. Season with pepper only (the haloumi is already salty enough).

Drain the pasta and place half of it in a 1.5-litre baking dish. Pour over half the cheese sauce and half the pork mince. Cover with remaining pasta and top with the remaining pork and finish with the sauce. Bake in the oven for 30 minutes until bubbling and golden.

Freeze for up to 3 months. Defrost overnight in the fridge and reheat thoroughly.

Pappardelle with chicken and crème fraîche sauce

Just 15 minutes and dinner's on the table... and very tasty it is too. I think the tarragon is essential but it's not always easy to buy fresh. Dried tarragon is actually very good, but if it must be dried be sure to stir into the sauce just before serving, rather than sprinkling on top. You can opt for turkey instead of chicken, and reduced-fat crème fraîche will save you a few calories too.

Serves 4 | Takes 5 minutes to make, 15 minutes to cook

375g pappardelle or tagliatelle
1 tbsp olive oil
400g minced chicken or turkey
2 shallots, finely chopped
1 clove garlic, crushed
150ml white wine
1 tbsp wholegrain mustard
200g crème fraiche
pinch grated nutmeg
salt and freshly ground black pepper
1 tbsp chopped fresh tarragon or 1 tsp dried tarragon

Cook the pasta in boiling water for 10–12 minutes until tender then drain well.

Heat the oil in a medium-sized frying pan and fry the mince, shallots and garlic until just browned. Add the wine and simmer for 10 minutes.

Reduce the heat and stir in the mustard, crème fraîche, nutmeg and seasoning. Serve poured over the pasta and sprinkle with the herbs.

Not suitable for freezing.

Creamy pork ragu

A fast and tasty midweek supper. You can use bacon if you don't have pancetta.

Serves 4 | Takes 10 minutes to make, 15 minutes to cook

500g minced pork
75g pancetta, diced
1 onion, finely chopped
1 carrot finely chopped
1 stick celery, finely chopped
1 clove garlic, crushed
150g wild mushrooms
150ml dry white wine
3 sage leaves, snipped
75g Parma ham, torn into strips
200ml mascarpone cheese
pinch ground nutmeg
400g tagliatelle or pasta shapes
**salt and freshly ground black
  pepper**
**2 tbsp chopped fresh parsley, to
  garnish**

Dry-fry the minced pork in a medium pan with the pancetta, chopped onion, carrot and celery for about 10 minutes until the vegetables are tender. Add the garlic, mushrooms and Parma ham and fry for another 3–4 minutes then pour on the wine and sprinkle with sage. Bring to the boil then simmer for 10 minutes.

Meanwhile, boil the pasta in lightly salted water for 11 minutes then drain well. Just before serving, stir the mascarpone into the mince and season with nutmeg, salt and pepper. Heat through without boiling and sprinkle with parsley just before serving with the cooked pasta.

Not suitable for freezing.

PORK

Stuffed pasta shells with crisp crumb topping

This is a hearty family dish that makes a great change from lasagne.

Serves 4 | Takes 30 minutes to make, 20 minutes to cook

For the meat sauce
300g conchiglioni (large pasta shells)
500g minced pork
1 onion, finely chopped
1 carrot, coarsely grated
1 stick celery, very finely chopped

For the tomato sauce
500ml passata
1–2 tsp dried oregano
1 clove,garlic, crushed

For the Béchamel sauce
25g butter
25g plain flour
150ml milk
salt and freshly ground black pepper
pinch grated nutmeg

For the cheese and breadcrumb topping
50g Parmesan cheese, grated
75g fresh breadcrumbs

Cook the pasta shells, as per pack instructions, until tender, then drain and allow to cool. Meanwhile, dry-fry the minced pork in a medium pan with the onion, carrot and celery for about 10 minutes until the vegetables are tender.

Pour the passata into the base of a 1.5-litre baking dish and stir in the oregano and garlic.

Set the oven to 180°C/160°C/gas 4.

To make the Béchamel, melt the butter in a small pan and add the flour. Stir well and cook over a medium heat for 1–2 minutes until thickened, then gradually beat in the milk a little at a time until smooth and thickened. Season with a little salt, pepper and nutmeg to taste. Stir the sauce into the pork mixture. Spoon a little of this mixture into each pasta shell and place them into the baking dish on top of the passata. Sprinkle with the Parmesan and breadcrumbs and bake for 20 minutes until golden and crisp.

Freeze without the crumb topping for up to 3 months. Defrost overnight in the fridge, add the crumbs and reheat thoroughly.

Chicken and pesto lasagne

This has become a bit of a favourite in our family – rich, hearty and smart enough to serve for a family gathering. You could just about stretch it to serve eight if you serve lots of green salad and garlic bread with it too (although in my house that means two families with youngish children – not eight hungry adults or teenagers!).

**Serves 6 | Takes 40 minutes
to prepare, 30 minutes to cook**

**500g minced chicken (or turkey)
1 onion, finely diced
1 clove garlic, crushed
6 tomatoes, roughly chopped
4 tbsp tomato purée
1 red pepper deseeded and cut
 into strips
$\frac{1}{2}$ tsp dried oregano
250g fresh egg lasagne sheets
225g washed spinach
250g ricotta cheese
4 tbsp basil pesto
150ml crème fraîche
125g Mozzarella cheese, grated
25g Parmesan cheese, grated
salt and freshly ground black
 pepper**

Dry-fry the minced chicken or turkey and onion for about 5 minutes until browned and the onion is beginning to soften. Add the garlic, tomatoes, tomato purée, red pepper and oregano. Cook for 2–3 minutes then pour over 150ml of water, bring to the boil then cover and simmer for 15 minutes. Taste and season with salt and pepper.

Meanwhile soak the lasagne sheets in boiling water or as directed on the packet.

Place the spinach in a colander over the sink and pour over boiling water until the spinach has wilted. Press gently to remove as much water as possible then place the spinach in a bowl with the ricotta and pesto. Mix well.

Set oven to 180°C/160°C fan/gas 4.

Place 2 sheets of lasagne in the base of a 2.5-litre ovenproof baking dish and pour over half the chicken mixture. Top with half the ricotta mixture. Add another 2 sheets of lasagne and most of the remaining chicken mixture, reserving a couple of tablespoons for the top.

Add the remaining ricotta mixture and top with the last two lasagne sheets. Spoon over the reserved chicken mixture then spread with crème fraîche and sprinkle with the Mozzarella and Parmesan. Bake for 25–30 minutes until piping hot in the centre and golden brown.

Freeze – but without the crème fraîche and cheese topping – for up to 3 months. Defrost overnight in the fridge and reheat thoroughly (this will take about 1 hour from cold).

Chicken and bacon pasta bake

This is a deliciously rich and creamy bake. Use reduced-fat crème fraîche and Mozzarella if you wish to make a lower-fat version. If you like, you could just serve the sauce along with the pasta, instead of baking it with the Mozzarella topping.

Serves 4 | Takes 15 minutes to make, 20 minutes to cook

**300g tagliatelle
500g minced turkey or chicken
1 onion, diced
6 rashers smoked back bacon, chopped
150g button mushrooms, sliced (optional)
2 tbsp fresh chopped parsley
2 tbsp plain flour
100g mild creamy blue cheese or 50g grated Mozzarella cheese and 50g grated Parmesan cheese
200ml milk
200ml crème fraîche
salt and freshly ground black pepper**

Boil the tagliatelle in lightly salted water for 8–10 minutes until just tender. It will continue to cook later. Then drain well.

Set the oven at 180°C/160°C fan/gas 4.

Dry-fry the minced turkey or chicken, onion and bacon for about 10 minutes until browned and the onion is tender. Add the mushrooms and parsley and continue to cook for a further 3–4 minutes, then sprinkle the flour over and cook for 1 minute. Gradually stir in the milk and crème fraîche, stirring until thick. Season to taste. Add the drained pasta and pour into a 1.5-litre baking dish. Top with the cheese and bake for 20 minutes.

Freeze for up to 3 months. Defrost overnight in the fridge and reheat thoroughly.

Gnocchi, lamb and spinach bake

A rich, cheesy and very quick midweek supper: one that all the family will enjoy.

Serves 4 | Takes 10 minutes to make, 15 minutes to cook

500g minced lamb
1 onion, finely diced
1 clove garlic, crushed
150g mushrooms, chopped
680g passata
500g readymade gnocchi
2 handfuls spinach, washed
150g Mozzarella cheese
50g Parmesan cheese, grated

In a large shallow pan, dry-fry the mince with the onion for 5 minutes until browned. Add the garlic and mushrooms and cook for a further 3–4 minutes. Pour over the passata and bring to the boil. Simmer for 10 minutes.

Cook the gnocchi according to pack instructions and when tender, drain and pour into a 1.5-litre baking dish.

Preheat the grill. Add the spinach to the mince and stir well. Pour over the gnocchi. Tear up the Mozzarella and scatter the Parmesan over the top. Grill for 2–3 minutes until the cheese has melted.

Not suitable for freezing.

Mushroom and chilli lamb gratinata

This is a simple, filling weekday supper. You can use any pasta shapes you have; gnocchi would be good too. Serve with a green salad.

Serve 4 | Takes 20 minutes to make, 15–20 minutes to cook

300g conchiglie or farfalle pasta shells
500g minced lamb
1 small onion, chopped
150g mushrooms, chopped
$\frac{1}{2}$ red chilli, deseeded and chopped
2 tsp dried oregano
1 tsp salt
1 tsp freshly ground black pepper
420g jar tomato pasta sauce
150ml red wine
50g black olives
2 handfuls spinach
50g fresh breadcrumbs
100g grated Mozzarella cheese
50g Parmesan cheese, grated

Set the oven to 180°C/160°C fan/gas 4.

Cook the pasta in lightly salted boiling water for 10 minutes until just tender (it will continue to cook further later).

Dry-fry the mince and onion in a large pan until browned. Add the mushrooms and chilli and fry for 3–4 minutes then add the oregano and seasoning. Add the tomato sauce, red wine and olives. Bring to the boil, then reduce the heat and simmer for 10 minutes.

Add the spinach and pasta to the pan and stir gently. Pour into a 1.5 litre baking dish and top with the grated Mozzarella and Parmesan. Bake for 15–20 minutes until golden and bubbling.

Freeze for up to 3 months. Defrost overnight in the fridge and reheat thoroughly.

HANDHELD HEAVEN

Between buns or bread, or secured onto skewers, the burger and the kebab can be so much more than boring barbecue standbys. There are myriad ways to fashion the most magical meal from a ball or patty of meat. With the right blend of herbs or spices, with vegetables thrown into the mix, and with salsas and sauces to bring some zing, you can create the most amazing casual launch or flame-grilled treat. Go on: get hands on!

Family hamburgers

You should always strive for the very best mince possible (see page 7 for tips on buying mince), but if you are limited to standard supermarket mince for your burger, this recipe will help deliver maximum flavour. Serve with any toppings you fancy, between burger buns, posh ciabatta rolls or just with chips.

Makes 4 | Takes 15 minutes to make, 8 minutes to cook

500g minced beef
1/2 onion, very finely chopped
2 tsp Worcestershire sauce
2 tsp Dijon mustard
1 tbsp tomato ketchup
30g fresh breadcrumbs
1 tsp salt
1/2 tsp freshly ground black pepper

To serve
burger buns, ciabatta rolls or chips
lettuce or rocket leaves
raw or fried sliced onions
sliced gherkins
sliced tomatoes
sliced Gruyère or Emmenthal cheese
American mustard, tomato ketchup or mayonnaise

Mix the beef with the onion, Worcestershire sauce, mustard, tomato ketchup and breadcrumbs. Mix together well with your hands then shape into 6 burgers and flatten so they are not too thick.

Preheat the grill or barbecue until hot. Cook burgers for 3–4 minutes on each side. See tips on cooking burgers (page 8).

Serve between split burger buns or ciabattta rolls and top with your choice of fillings.

Variations (cook as main recipe):

Teriyaki burger
Brush the burgers generously with teriyaki sauce while cooking, for a delicious sticky glaze.

Cheese burger
Add 100g of grated Cheddar cheese to the mixture and top with a slice of processed cheese or a melting cheese such as Emmenthal or Gruyère.

Mediterranean burger
Add 1 teaspoon of dried oregano and 100g of chopped sun-dried tomatoes to the mixture.

Harissa burger
Mix the beef with 1 teaspoon of toasted cumin seeds, 1/2 teaspoon of ground cinnamon and 1 teaspoon of harissa paste.

Chilli burger
Add 1 small finely chopped red pepper, 1 small finely chopped red chilli, 1 clove of crushed garlic and 1 teaspoon of ground cumin.

To freeze, layer the uncooked burgers between squares of baking parchment and pack in a plastic bag. Freeze for up to 1 month, defrost in the fridge for 4–5 hours before cooking as above.

Pork and apple burgers

I particularly like using crumbs made from pitta bread for this recipe; they are somehow more like rusk and absorb the fat and moisture really well in the burgers.

Makes 6 burgers | Takes 15 minutes to make, 15 minutes to cook

1 crisp eating apple (Braeburns are ideal), grated
400g minced pork
1/2 tsp freshly ground black pepper
1 small onion, finely diced
75g breadcrumbs (use day-old bread or pitta bread)
1 tsp salt
6 burger buns, to serve

Combine the apple, pork, onion, salt, pepper and breadcrumbs. Mix well together with your hands then shape into 6 burgers and flatten so they are not too thick.

Preheat the grill or barbecue until hot. Grill or fry for 5–6 minutes on each side (see tips on cooking burgers, page 8) until no longer pink in the centre. Allow to rest for 5 minutes before serving with burger buns. Add salad and relishes to serve, if liked.

Variations (cook as main recipe):

Tomato and paprika burgers
Instead of the apple, add 25g of finely chopped chorizo, tomato purée and a pinch of smoked paprika to the minced pork and top with grated cheese.

Thai pork burgers
Instead of the apple and onion, mix 3 finely chopped spring onions, a small bunch of chopped coriander, 1–2 tablespoons of Thai red curry paste and a dash of Thai fish sauce (nam pla) into the mince and serve with sweet chilli sauce.

Sweet chilli burgers
Instead of the apple, add 2 tablespoons of sweet chilli sauce to the mince with 1 clove of crushed garlic and a small handful of chopped fresh coriander leaves.

To freeze, layer the uncooked burgers between squares of baking parchment and pack in a plastic bag. Freeze for up to 1 month. Defrost in the fridge for 4–5 hours before cooking as above.

Lamb and feta cheese burgers with fresh pea and mint sauce

These make a great change from standard barbecue fare. Make in advance and then chill them until ready to cook. The pea and mint sauce can be made up to an hour before serving too.

Makes 6 burgers | Takes 15 minutes to make, 12 minutes to cook

500g minced lamb
¹/₂ onion, finely diced
10g fresh mint, finely chopped
1 clove garlic, crushed
¹/₂ tsp salt
freshly ground black pepper
50g Feta cheese

For the fresh pea and mint sauce
1 tbsp clear honey
1 tbsp white wine
1 tbsp white wine vinegar
1 tsp golden caster sugar
25g fresh mint
150g peas
ciabatta rolls, to serve

First, make the sauce. Place the honey, wine, white wine vinegar and sugar in a small pan. Bring to the boil, boil for 1 minute, then pour into a jug and allow to cool. Strip the leaves off the mint, chop very finely and stir into the cooled vinegar mixture. Boil the peas in water for 2–3 minutes, drain, crush lightly with a potato masher and cool a little before adding to the mint sauce. Serve the lamb burgers with the mint sauce.

Meanwhile, mix the lamb with the onion, mint, garlic, salt and plenty of black pepper. Crumble in the feta cheese and mix well. With damp hands, shape into 6 burgers and flatten well. Cook for 5–6 minutes on each side until tender and cooked through. See tips on cooking burgers (page 8).

To freeze, layer the uncooked burgers between squares of baking parchment and pack in a plastic bag. Freeze for up to 1 month. Defrost in the fridge for 4–5 hours before cooking as above.

Chilli chicken burgers

Chicken burgers are a lighter, healthier alternative to beef and can be jazzed up in lots of great ways. Turkey can be substituted just as well.

Makes 4 burgers | Takes 10 minutes to make, 12 minutes to cook

500g minced chicken (or turkey)
1 onion, very finely chopped
2 cloves garlic, crushed
2 tbsp sweet chilli sauce
3 tbsp chopped fresh coriander
 leaves
3 tbsp fresh breadcrumbs
1 egg yolk
$\frac{1}{2}$ tsp salt and freshly ground
 black pepper
4 crusty rolls, sliced tomatoes and
 shredded lettuce, to serve

Place the mince in a bowl with the onion, garlic, chilli sauce, coriander leaves, breadcrumbs and egg yolk. Add the salt and plenty of black pepper, then shape into 4 burgers. Preheat the grill or barbecue until hot. Flatten well then, grill or barbecue for 5–6 minutes on each side until the juices run clear. (see tips on cooking burgers, page 8).

Serve between burger buns with lettuce and tomatoes.

Variations (cook as main recipe):

Turkey and chorizo burgers with cheese and sundried tomato melt

Omit the sweet chilli sauce and coriander from the basic recipe and use $\frac{1}{2}$ teaspoon of smoked mild paprika and 50g of very finely chopped chorizo sausage instead.

Very finely chop 50g of sunblush tomatoes and mash into 100g of full-fat cream cheese. Dollop on top of the cooked burgers.

Serve between slices of ciabatta bread with strips of roasted red peppers and rocket leaves.

Thai chicken burgers

Omit the sweet chilli sauce from the basic recipe. Add 2cm of grated fresh root ginger, 1 chopped red chilli and 1 finely chopped stick of lemongrass. Serve with lettuce and spring onions.

To freeze, layer the uncooked burgers between squares of baking parchment and pack in a plastic bag. Freeze for up to 1 month. Defrost in the fridge for 4–5 hours before cooking as above.

Herby lamb burgers

I love lamb burgers – more than I do beef burgers. They have a lovely sweet taste and are great stuffed into warm pitta bread with salad, and just as nice served more conventionally with buns and chips, as here. This is a great basic lamb burger recipe.

Makes 6 burgers | Takes 15 minutes to make, 15 minutes to cook

500g minced lamb
30g fresh breadcrumbs
1 small onion, very finely chopped
3 tbsp chopped fresh parsley
1 tsp chopped fresh rosemary
1 tsp salt
1 tsp freshly ground black pepper
6 burger buns or chips, to serve

Mix the minced lamb with the breadcrumbs, onion, 1 tablespoon of the parsley and rosemary. Season well and shape into 6 burgers (make triangular ones for a change if liked). Roll the edge of the burgers in the remaining parsley. Place on a plate and chill for 30 minutes if you have the time.

Preheat the grill or barbecue until hot. Cook burgers for 5–6 minutes on each side (see tips on cooking burgers, page 8) until no longer pink in the centre. Allow to rest for 5 minutes before serving with burger buns or oven chips.

Variations (cook as main recipe):

Moroccan-spiced burgers
Omit the rosemary and mix the minced lamb with 1 tablespoon of chopped parsley, 1 tablespoons of chopped mint, a pinch each of cinnamon, allspice and mace and $1/2$ teaspoon of cumin and shape into burgers. Serve with hummous.

Italian burgers
Mix 1 tablespoons sun-dried tomato paste into the mince mixture with 50g of chopped sunblush tomatoes and 1 teaspoon of dried oregano. Serve with ciabatta rolls.

Middle Eastern burgers
Mix 1–2 tablespoons of harissa paste into the mince with 2 tablespoons of toasted pine nuts.

Rogan Josh burgers
Mix 1 crushed clove of garlic and 1–2 tablespoons of Rogan Josh curry paste into the mince and serve with naan breads.

To freeze, layer the uncooked burgers between squares of baking parchment and pack in a plastic bag. Freeze for up to 1 month, defrost in the fridge for 4–5 hours before cooking as above.

LAMB

Korma kebabs with cumin raita

These fragrantly spiced kebabs always go down a treat at barbecues but are just as good grilled for supper. They are great stuffed into pitta breads or served with salad. They're even good cold the next day too!

Serves 4 | Takes 20 minutes to make, 15 minutes to cook

450g minced pork or lamb
50g fine breadcrumbs
1 onion, finely diced
1 tsp chillies, finely chopped
1 tsp korma curry powder
3cm piece fresh root ginger, grated
1 tsp ground cinnamon
1 tsp ground coriander
2 cloves garlic, crushed
1 tsp salt and $^1/_4$ tsp ground black pepper

For the cumin raita
$^1/_2$ tsp ground cumin
300ml natural yoghurt
4 tomatoes, diced
$^1/_4$ cucumber, diced
$^1/_4$ red onion, diced
naan bread, to serve

You will need 8 metal skewers, or 8 wooden skewers soaked in cold water for at least 10 minutes

Place all ingredients for the kebabs in a food processor and whiz until it binds together into a ball. Divide into 8 and shape into 8 sausages around metal or wooden skewers.

Preheat the grill to high, then grill for 12–15 minutes, turning occasionally until golden and cooked through (alternatively, bake at 200°C/180°C fan/gas 6 for 20 minutes).

Meanwhile, make the raita. Mix the cumin, yoghurt, tomatoes, cucumber and red onion together and serve with the kebabs and naan bread.

Pork and apricot patties with sweet potato wedges

These make a great midweek meal served with sweet potato wedges. Oven chips and salad also make for a fitting accompaniment. They are also good barbecued too.

Makes 8 patties | Takes 20 minutes to make, plus chilling, 15 minutes to cook

1 tbsp sunflower oil
1/2 onion, finely diced
3 rashers streaky bacon, finely chopped
1 clove garlic, crushed
75g wholemeal bread
handful fresh parsley, finely chopped
450g minced pork
100g ready-to-eat dried apricots, finely chopped
1/2 tsp salt
freshly ground black pepper

For the sweet potato wedges
2–3 sweet potatoes (peeled or unpeeled), quartered and then cut into 2–3 long wedges
vegetable oil, to drizzle
pinch salt and freshly ground black pepper or cajun seasoning

If serving with the sweet potato wedges, make these first. Spread the sweet potato wedges on a baking tray and drizzle with a little vegetable oil. Sprinkle with seasoning or Cajun spices and roast at 220°C/200°C fan/gas 7 for about 25–35 minutes or until tender.

Meanwhile, make the burgers. Heat the oil in a frying pan and fry the onion and bacon over a low heat until the onion has softened. Add the garlic and fry for 1 minute. Cut the crusts off the bread and discard. Place the bread and parsley in a food processor, whiz to make crumbs then add the cooked onion and bacon, pork, apricots, salt and plenty of ground black pepper. Whiz until well mixed. Shape the mixture into 8 oval flat burgers or patties and place on a plate. Chill for 30 minutes if you have the time.

Preheat the grill to high. Grill the patties for about 6–8 minutes on each side until golden and cooked through. Serve with sweet potato wedges.

To freeze the patties, layer the uncooked patties between squares of baking parchment and pack in a plastic bag. Freeze for up to 1 month, defrost in the fridge for 4–5 hours before cooking as above.

Venison burgers with root vegetable crisps and blue cheese

This recipe is taken from the book, *Game for Gourmets* (Swan Hill Press) which was sponsored by the Countryside Alliance's Game-to-Eat campaign. The recipes in the book are all from chefs that are passionate about game. This recipe is from the acclaimed gastropub chef, Neil Dowson. Readymade vegetable crisps are perfectly adequate, but homemade ones will really help this dish to sing!

Serves 4 | Takes 20–30 minutes to make plus chilling, and 10 minutes to cook

600g coarsely minced venison
1 red onion, finely chopped
1 tsp chopped fresh thyme leaves
sea salt
freshly ground black pepper
4 slices blue cheese

For the root vegetable crisps
200ml vegetable oil
1 parsnip
2 carrots
1 celeriac
200ml vegetable oil, for frying

4 burger buns, toasted
salad and mustard, to serve

Mix the mince, onion and thyme together, adding salt and pepper to season. If you wish, fry a small piece of the mix and taste it to make sure that the seasoning is just right for you. Divide the mixture into four patties and place in the fridge for a couple of hours to firm up.

Finely slice the root vegetables (use a mandolin if you have one). Heat the vegetable oil until a cube of bread sizzles and begins to turn golden brown almost immediately. Fry the sliced root vegetables until crisp. Drain and season with salt. Set aside on paper towels.

Preheat the grill to high. Heat a frying pan with a little oil and fry the burgers for 4–5 minutes on each side, longer if you like them well done. Place the burgers on the grill, add a slice of blue cheese and brown under the grill. Serve the burgers in toasted buns with root vegetable crisps, salad and mustard.

To freeze, layer the uncooked burgers between squares of baking parchment and pack in a plastic bag. Freeze for up to 1 month, defrost in the fridge for 4–5 hours before cooking as above.

Peanut pork kebabs

These are a great favourite with kids. Serve them with sweet chilli sauce, rice and a green salad.

Serves 4 | Takes 15 minutes
to make, 10–12 minutes to cook

3 tbsp roasted peanuts
350g minced pork
1 tbsp soy sauce
4 spring onions, very finely
chopped
3 tbsp creamed coconut
1 tsp korma curry powder
¹/₂ tsp salt
sweet chilli sauce, rice and green
salad, to serve

You will need 4 metal skewers, or
4 wooden skewers soaked in cold
water for at least 10 minutes

Place the peanuts in a food processor and whiz until finely chopped. Add the pork, soy sauce, spring onions, creamed coconut, curry powder and salt and whiz quickly to bind the mixture together.

Turn out and with damp hands, shape the mixture into 12 small meatballs. Flatten each slightly and thread 3 onto each skewer.

Preheat the grill to high. Cook under the grill for 5–6 minutes on each side. Serve with sweet chilli sauce, rice and a green salad.

To freeze, layer the uncooked burgers between squares of baking parchment and pack in a plastic bag. Freeze for up to 1 month, defrost in the fridge for 4–5 hours before cooking as above.

Moroccan kofta wraps with onion salad

Rich and spicy, these are great for a barbecue or summer supper.

Serves 6 | Takes 25 minutes
to make, 15 minutes to cook

450g minced beef
1 small onion, finely diced
$\frac{1}{2}$ tsp ground cumin
1 tsp harissa paste
small handful chopped fresh
coriander
$\frac{1}{2}$ tsp salt and plenty of freshly
ground black pepper

For the onion salad
1 small red onion
juice 1 lemon
small handful chopped fresh
coriander leaves
sea salt
flatbreads, mango chutney, lime
wedges and Greek yoghurt
sprinkled with paprika to serve

You will need 6 metal skewers, or
6 wooden skewers soaked in cold
water for at least 10 minutes

Place the beef in a mixing bowl with the onion, cumin, harissa and coriander. Season well and mix with your hands until well blended. With damp hands, divide the mixture into 6 and shape each into a long sausage over the skewers. Chill if you have the time.

To make the onion salad, cut the onion as thinly as possible and mix with the lemon juice, coriander and a little salt. Chill until ready to serve.

Preheat the grill to high. Cook the koftas under the grill or on the barbecue for about 12–15 minutes, turning every 2–3 minutes until they are no longer pink in the centre.

Remove the skewers and place the koftas onto flatbreads with a spoonful of onion salad, a little mango chutney and some Greek yoghurt. Roll up and enjoy!

To freeze, layer the uncooked burgers between squares of baking parchment and pack in a plastic bag. Freeze for up to 1 month. Defrost in the fridge for 4–5 hours before cooking as above.

Korean beef in lettuce

A refreshing, light summer supper or starter.

Serves 4 | Takes 5 minutes
to make, 10 minutes to cook

1 Romaine lettuce
400g minced beef
250g mushrooms, diced
3 tbsp hoisin sauce
juice 1 lime
1 red chilli, finely chopped
small handful chopped fresh
  coriander

Break the lettuce into individual leaves and arrange on a platter. Dry-fry the mince and mushrooms for 5 minutes until the mince is browned and cooked through. Add the hoisin sauce, lime juice and chilli and fry for 2–3 minutes. Stir in the coriander leaves at the end of cooking. Serve in a bowl. To eat, spoon a little into each lettuce leaf, roll up and bite.

Not suitable for freezing.

WONDERS OF THE WORLD

Look east for fast stir-fries and creamy curries, Middle Eastern pilafs and Thai noodles. Go west for glorious goulashes, moussakas, enchiladas and American meat loaf. Spicy, flavoursome, simple-to-make old and new recipes that will perk up midweek mealtimes and bring a touch of the exotic to suppers for friends.

Middle Eastern nut pilaf

This is delicately spiced and delicious. Don't be tempted to use oil instead of butter as you need the richness of butter for this dish and it also creates a lovely crust on the bottom of the pan. Use up whatever nuts you have in the cupboard.

Serves 4 | Takes 10 minutes to make, 10 minutes to cook

pinch saffron threads
400ml hot chicken stock
25g butter
1 onion, chopped
250g minced chicken or turkey
1 cinnamon stick
2cm piece fresh root ginger, cut into matchsticks (optional)
8 green cardamom pods, cracked
3 tbsp sultanas
200g basmati rice
100g mixed nuts: pistachios, pine nuts, pecans, cashews

Place the saffron in a measuring jug and pour on the hot stock. Heat the butter in a medium pan and fry the onion and mince for 5 minutes until the onion has softened and the mince is browned. Add the cinnamon, ginger, cardamom, sultanas and rice. Stir well then pour over the saffron-scented stock. Bring to the boil then cover, reduce the heat and simmer for 10 minutes undisturbed until the rice is cooked and all the stock has been absorbed. Remove from the heat and leave for 5 minutes then turn out of the pan scraping the lovely buttery crust from the base of the pan. Sprinkle with the nuts and serve.

Leftovers can be stored for 1 day only and reheated thoroughly. Not suitable for freezing.

Creole rice

This is based on a jambalaya recipe and is great, filling family food. Make the meal stretch even further by adding sweetcorn, peas, or chopped courgettes. I prefer chorizo sausage (buy the small whole cooked sausages rather than the sliced meat), but my children prefer frankfurters. Choose whatever your family likes best.

Serves 4–6 | Takes 10 minutes to make, 15 minutes to cook

2 tbsp olive oil
1 onion, diced
1 clove garlic, crushed
200g minced chicken, turkey or
　　pork
125g long grain rice
400g can chopped tomatoes
150g roasted red peppers
　　(from a jar), chopped
600ml vegetable or chicken stock
pinch allspice
pinch smoked paprika
1 bay leaf
100g frankfurters or chorizo
　　sausage, thickly sliced
salt and freshly ground black
　　pepper
chopped fresh parsley, to garnish

Heat the oil in a large frying pan and fry the onion, garlic and mince for 5 minutes until browned and tender. Add the rice and cook for 1 minute then add the tomatoes, red peppers and stock. Season with salt, pepper, allspice and paprika and add the bay leaf. Bring to the boil then add the frankfurter or chorizo sausage, reduce the heat and simmer gently for 15 minutes until the rice is tender and most of the liquid has been absorbed. Serve sprinkled with the fresh parsley.

Leftovers can be stored for 1 day only and reheated thoroughly.

Not suitable for freezing.

CHICKEN

Baked peppers

Long red Ramiro peppers have a sweeter richer flavour than bell peppers, but you can of course use bell peppers if you prefer. This mixture also works well packed into big beef tomatoes or aubergines.

Serves 4 | Takes 25 minutes to make, 25 minutes to cook

300g minced beef
1 garlic clove, crushed
1 courgette, grated
1 carrot, grated
400g can chopped tomatoes
2 tbsp tomato purée
2 tsp balsamic vinegar
1 tsp sugar
4 long Ramiro peppers, halved and deseeded
4 salad onions, finely sliced
green salad, to serve

Set the oven to 190°C/170°C fan/gas 5.

Dry-fry the mince in a large pan cooking it for a few minutes until browned. Add the garlic, courgette and carrot. Add the canned tomatoes, tomato purée, balsamic vinegar and sugar. Bring to the boil, then reduce the heat and simmer for 15 minutes. Taste and adjust the seasoning.

Arrange the pepper halves in a baking dish or roasting tin, cut sides up. Spoon the mince mixture into them. Cover with foil and bake for 25 minutes.

Serve 2 pepper halves per person. Sprinkle them with chopped salad onions and serve with plenty of green salad on the side.

These can be stored for 1 day and reheated thoroughly. Not suitable for freezing.

Beef enchiladas

This makes a great relaxed supper for friends. Serve with a big bowl of grated cheese, an avocado salsa (page 120) or guacamole, sour cream and shredded lettuce, as well as lime wedges and a bottle of Tabasco sauce (for those who like to add a splash of heat to their enchiladas).

Serves 4 | Takes 30 minutes to make, 5 minutes to cook

500g minced beef
1 onion, finely chopped
1 clove garlic, crushed
400g can chopped tomatoes
3 tbsp tomato purée
$\frac{1}{2}$ tsp dried oregano
$\frac{1}{2}$ tsp ground cumin
$\frac{1}{2}$ tsp chilli powder or to taste
8 flour tortillas
150g Cheddar cheese, grated
$\frac{1}{2}$ small red chilli, sliced
1 tbsp chopped fresh parsley

Avocado Salsa or guacamole, sour cream, shredded lettuce and lime wedges to serve

Dry-fry the minced beef and onion in a medium pan for about 5 minutes until browned. Add the garlic and fry for 1 minute then add the tomatoes, tomato purée, oregano, cumin, chilli powder and a little salt. Bring to the boil then cover and simmer for 15 minutes.

Set the grill to hot.

Warm the flour tortillas in a frying pan. Spread a little mince over half of each tortilla, roll up each one and place together in a 2-litre baking dish. Top with grated cheese, chilli and parsley and grill until golden. Serve with avocado salsa or guacamole, sour cream, shredded lettuce and lime wedges.

This can be made in advance, chilled in the fridge and reheated thoroughly. Not suitable for freezing.

Chimichangas

Chimichangas are basically fried, filled tortilla parcels and they make a great TV dinner. My family love them. For a main meal they like two each so double the recipe if you have hungry mouths to feed. I like to serve them with a simple avocado salsa.

**Serves 6 as a light lunch |
Takes 30 minutes to make,
12 minutes to cook**

**1 tbsp sunflower oil
500g minced turkey or chicken
1 red onion, sliced
1 clove garlic, crushed
1/2 red chilli, finely chopped
1/2 green pepper, sliced
6 tomatoes, chopped
pinch ground cumin
juice 1 lime
2 tbsp chopped fresh coriander
  leaves
6 flour tortillas
salt and freshly ground black
  pepper
6 tbsp vegetable oil, for frying**

**For the avocado salsa
1 avocado, de-stoned
100g cherry tomatoes, chopped
1/2 small red onion, finely chopped
1/2 red chilli, finely chopped
juice 1 lime
2 tbsp chopped coriander**

**shredded lettuce and sour cream,
  to serve**

Make the salsa first if serving alongside the chimichangas. Scoop out the avocado flesh and mash roughly. Add the tomatoes, onion, chilli, lime juice and coriander and chill until ready to serve.

Heat the oil in a medium pan and fry the mince and red onion for about 5–6 minutes until the meat is browned and the onion tender. Add the garlic, chopped chilli, green pepper and tomatoes. Season well with salt, pepper and cumin. Cover and simmer over a low heat for 15 minutes then stir in the lime juice and coriander.

Place a generous spoonful of the chicken mixture in the centre of each tortilla. Fold 2 sides over the filling then fold the other sides over like a parcel.

Heat the oil in a deep frying pan (it's hot enough when a cube of bread sizzles and turns golden almost instantly). Add two of the chimichangas and fry for 3–4 minutes, turning after 2 minutes until each side is golden brown and crisp. Remove from the pan, place onto paper towel and keep warm whilst you repeat with the remaining chimichangas.

Serve with the avocado salsa, sour cream and lettuce.

The mince can be made in advance, but don't roll in tortillas until ready to cook. Not suitable for freezing.

Quesadillas

Use beef or lamb mince to make this fast and fabulous TV supper.

Serves 4 | Takes 5 minutes to make, 10 minutes to cook

500g minced beef
1 onion, thinly sliced
1 red pepper, deseeded and sliced
1 clove garlic, crushed
$\frac{1}{2}$ tsp paprika
pinch chilli powder
1 tbsp sunflower oil
8 flour tortillas
4 tbsp tomato salsa (see below)
6 spring onions, chopped
150g Cheddar cheese, grated
50g grated Mozzarella cheese
fresh coriander leaves
salt and freshly ground black
   pepper

For the tomato salsa
6 tomatoes, deseeded and roughly
   chopped
$\frac{1}{2}$ red onion, finely sliced
2 tbsp finely chopped fresh
   coriander
$\frac{1}{2}$ red chilli, deseeded and finely
   sliced
juice $\frac{1}{2}$ lime
olive oil
salt and freshly ground black
   pepper

Make the salsa first. Mix the tomatoes, onion, coriander and chilli together with the lime juice and a little drizzle of olive oil. Season and chill until ready to use.

Dry-fry the mince and onion in a large frying pan until the meat is browned and the onions are getting tender. Add the red pepper and garlic, and cook for a further 5 minutes. Stir in the paprika and chilli powder with a little salt and black pepper to taste.

Lightly grease a large frying pan and add a tortilla. Top with a little of the mince mixture, a spoonful of salsa, some chopped spring onions, a good sprinkling of cheese and coriander. Place a second tortilla on top. Cook over a medium heat for 1–2 minutes then, using a fish slice, flip the tortilla over (or slide onto a plate then flip back into the pan). Cook the remaining tortillas and serve cut into wedges with more tomato salsa alongside.

Variation: Beefy nachos with salsa

Cook the mince as for the Quesadillas recipe above. Arrange plenty of tortilla chips on heatproof plates. Spoon some mince on top, sprinkle with grated cheese and grill for 2–3 minutes under a hot grill until the cheese melts. Chop an avocado into the tomato salsa and serve on top of the nachos. Serve with lime wedges.

Not suitable for freezing.

Paprika-spiced mince with cheesy polenta

On a cold winter's evening there's nothing nicer than a plate of mince with mash, but try serving this spicy mince with cheesey polenta for a change.

Serves 4 | Takes 30 minutes to make, 20 minutes to cook

500g minced beef
1 onion, finely chopped
1 stick celery, chopped
1 red or green pepper, deseeded and diced
1 clove garlic, crushed
100g chorizo sausage, diced
400g can chopped tomatoes
3 tbsp tomato purée
1 tsp chopped fresh or $^{1}/_{2}$ tsp dried oregano
$^{1}/_{2}$ tsp ground cumin
2 tsp sweet mild paprika

For the cheesey polenta
150g instant polenta
2 pinches dried crushed chillies
1 pinch dried oregano
salt and freshly gound black pepper
100g Cheddar cheese

Dry-fry the minced beef in a large pan with the onion for about 5 minutes until the mince is browned and the onion is becoming tender. Add the celery, pepper, garlic and chorizo sausage and fry for a further 5 minutes to soften the vegetables. Stir in the tomatoes, tomato purée, oregano, cumin and paprika and bring to the boil. Cover and simmer for 20 minutes.

Meanwhile, cook the polenta as directed on the pack, adding plenty of boiling water to give a soft, creamy, quite wet mash. Add the chillies, oregano and plenty of seasoning. Stir in the cheese just before serving. Serve the polenta mash with the mince on top. Sprinkle with extra dried crushed chilli and oregano before serving, if liked.

This can be made in advance, chilled in the fridge and reheated thoroughly. Freeze for up to 1 month. Defrost in the fridge overnight and reheat thoroughly.

Cuban beef picadillo

This is an adaptation of a recipe from *Eating Cuban* by Beverly Cox and Martin Jacobs (Stewart, Tabori and Chang). It is a piquant, almost sweet and sour mince that is totally fab served with rice or used as a filling for tortillas. I've also given the recipe for Rice 'n' Black Beans, which are traditionally served with this dish, but you need to soak the beans overnight if using.

Serves 6 | Takes 20 minutes to prepare, 20 minutes to cook (plus overnight soaking and 30 minutes cook time for the rice and beans)

500g steak mince
2 onions, finely diced
1 green pepper, deseeded and
   diced
2 cloves garlic, crushed
400g can chopped tomatoes
50g sliced pimento stuffed olives
   (optional)
50g raisins
1 tbsp capers in brine, drained
3 tbsp white wine vinegar
$\frac{1}{2}$ tsp ground cumin
$\frac{1}{2}$ tsp dried oregano
salt and a pinch of sugar to taste
black beans and rice
3 rashers back bacon, diced
$\frac{1}{2}$ onion, finely diced
$\frac{1}{2}$ green pepper

for the rice and beans
75g black beans, soaked overnight
   and drained
200g long grain rice
$\frac{1}{2}$ onion, chopped
1 tbsp sunflower oil
2 cloves garlic, crushed
1 tsp ground cumin
pinch ground cinnamon
salt and freshly ground black
   pepper
small handful coriander, chopped

Dry-fry the mince and onion in a medium pan until browned and the onion is beginning to soften. Add the green pepper and garlic and fry for 2–3 minutes then add the remaining ingredients and simmer for 20 minutes until the meat is tender.

Rinse the beans thoroughly in cold water and place in a large saucepan, cover them with fresh cold water and bring them up to boiling point and boil rapidly for 10 minutes. Then turn down the heat and simmer for 30 minutes until tender.

Cook the rice in boiling salted water for 10–12 minutes then drain.

Fry the onion in the oil for 5 minutes until tender and golden brown, then add the garlic, cumin and cinnamon. Stir for 1 minute then add the rice, drained beans, seasoning and chopped coriander. Serve with the beef.

Freeze the meat suace and the rice and beans separately for up to 1 month. Defrost overnight and reheat thoroughly.

Variation: papa rellenas

You can also use this meat filling in *papa rellenas* (meat-stuffed potatoes). These are very popular all over Latin America as a snack from street cafés, and I'm sure you'll love them too. They're a bit tricky, but well worth the effort. Spoon a little of the meat sauce into a hollow ball of cold mashed potato mixture and mould to enclose the meat. Dip in beaten egg and breadcrumbs and deep-fry until golden.

Lamb tagine

I love the fiery flavours of the harissa with the sweetness of the apricots in this dish. Top with whole toasted or flaked almonds too if liked.

Serves 4 | Takes 15 minutes to make, 30 minutes to cook

500g lean minced lamb
1 onion, chopped
2 cloves garlic, crushed
1–2 tbsp harissa paste
400g can chopped tomatoes with herbs
500ml tomato passata
100g ready-to-eat apricots, quartered
420g can chick peas, drained
250g butternut squash, chopped into small cubes
350g couscous
salt and freshly ground black pepper

Dry-fry the lamb and onions in a large pan until the meat is browned all over and the onions are becoming tender. Add the remaining ingredients (except the couscous). Bring to the boil then reduce the heat and simmer for 30 minutes until the meat and butternut squash are tender. Taste and season with salt and pepper if necessary.

Pour 400ml boiling water over the couscous. Cover with clingfilm and leave for 5 minutes until the grains have swollen and serve with the lamb.

Freeze for up to 1 month. Defrost overnight and reheat thoroughly.

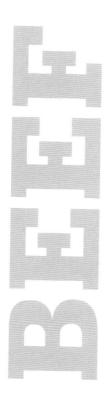

Goulash soup

This is a traditional recipe once served all over the former Austro-Hungarian empire and is still very popular in the Austrian mountains as a warming winter lunch. Although stewing beef is traditionally used, minced beef does make for a much quicker version.

Serves 6–8 | Takes 20 minutes to make, 20 minutes to cook

2 tbsp olive oil
500g minced beef
1 onion, chopped
1½ tsp caraway seeds
3 tbsp sweet paprika
300ml beef stock
3 garlic cloves, minced
1 baking potato
1 parsnip, chopped
1 carrot, chopped
1 stick celery, chopped
1 green pepper, deseeded and diced
400g can chopped tomatoes
6 tablespoons sour cream and paprika, to garnish

Heat the oil in large pan and fry the beef for 5 minutes until browned. Add the onion and caraway seeds and sauté until the onion begins to soften. Add the paprika and stir for 1 minute then pour over the beef stock. Bring to the boil, then add the garlic and all the vegetables and tomatoes, simmer for 15–20 minutes until the vegetables are tender. Serve with soured cream and a sprinkle of paprika if liked.

This dish is even better if made a day in advance then reheated until piping hot. Freeze for up to 1 month.

American meat loaf

This is a great family meal which can be made in advance and chilled in the fridge either before or after cooking. Serve it hot with mashed potato (add crushed sweetcorn and chopped chilli to the mash) or serve it cold with salad and bread to make a tasty lunch. For a simpler version, use a half-beef, half-pork mince mixture and flavour with a tablespoon of Worcestershire sauce, a teaspoon of Dijon mustard (instead of the chilli, cumin and paprika) and add extra carrots instead of red pepper.

Serves 6 | Takes 20 minutes to make, 45 minutes to cook

1 small onion, quartered
1 carrot, cut into chunks
75g mushrooms
1 clove garlic, crushed
1½ tbsp chopped fresh flat leaf parsley
1 tbsp sunflower oil
50g fresh bread, crusts removed
250g reduced-fat minced pork
250g steak mince
1 roasted red pepper (from a jar will do), cut into 1cm dice
½ red chilli, deseeded and finely chopped
1 tsp salt
1 tsp freshly ground black pepper
¼ tsp ground cumin
¼ tsp hot smoked paprika
grating of nutmeg
2 tbsp tomato purée
1 egg, beaten
200g cherry tomatoes
green salad, to serve

Place the onion, carrot, mushrooms, garlic and 1 tablespoon of the parsley in a food processor and whizz until finely chopped (if you don't have a food processor, chop everything finely with a knife).

Set the oven to 180°C/160°C fan/gas 4.

Heat the oil in a frying pan and fry the chopped vegetables for 5 minutes until tender. Place the bread in a food processor and whizz to crumbs. Place the vegetables in a large mixing bowl and add the breadcrumbs and the pork and steak mince along with the red pepper, chilli, salt, pepper, cumin, paprika, nutmeg and tomato purée. Add the egg and mix everything with your hands until well blended.

Turn the mixture into a 500g non-stick or greased loaf tin and cover with baking parchment and foil. Seal well, then place in a roasting tin and pour hot water into the roasting tin to come halfway up the sides of the loaf tin. Bake for 45 minutes until firm. Place the cherry tomatoes on a baking tray and bake for the last 5 minutes of cooking time. To serve hot, drain off any liquid (it can be used to make gravy) and slice the meatloaf. Serve with the cherry tomatoes and the remaining ½ tablespoon of parlsey sprinkled over. If serving cold, allow the meatloaf to cool completely then chill overnight, then turn out and serve with the cherry tomatoes and a simple green salad.

Not suitable for freezing.

Lamb moussaka

A rich and traditional Greek dish of minced lamb layered up with moist aubergines. Crumbled feta cheese is probably more traditional in the sauce but I like the flavour of Gruyère. This dish is even better if made a day ahead, chilled and reheated. This dish also works really well replacing the lamb with a mixture of venison and beef mince.

Serves 6 | Takes 45 minutes to make, 35 minutes to cook

225g potatoes
4 tbsp olive oil
1 large onion, finely chopped
500g minced lamb
100ml full-bodied red wine
400g can chopped tomatoes
4 tbsp tomato purée
150ml lamb stock
3 tbsp chopped fresh parsley
1 tbsp dried oregano
1 tsp ground cinnamon
2 large aubergines

For the sauce
40g butter
40g plain flour
600ml milk
100g Gruyère cheese, grated
3 eggs

Boil the potatoes for 10 minutes then drain and allow to cool and cut into 5mm slices.

Meanwhile, heat 1 tablespoon of the oil in a large pan and fry the onions for about 5 minutes until tender. Add the lamb and fry for 5 minutes until browned. Pour on the wine and bring to the boil. Cook until the wine has reduced by half then add the tomatoes and tomato purée, stock, herbs and cinnamon. Bring back to the boil then simmer for 20 minutes.

Preheat the grill to hot. Cut the aubergine widthways into 5mm slices. Brush all over with oil and grill each side for about 5 minutes until golden brown, brushing with oil occasionally. Drain the aubergines on kitchen paper to absorb some of the oil.

To make the sauce, melt the butter in a medium pan and add the flour, cook for 1 minute until thickened, then very gradually pour in the milk, stirring until smooth and thickened. Allow to cool for 5 minutes then stir in the cheese and eggs.

Set oven to 180°C/160°C fan/gas 4. Spoon a third of the mince mixture into the base of a 2-litre baking dish. Cover with potato slices then two layers each of mince and aubergines, finishing with a layer of aubergine on top. Pour over the sauce and bake for 35 minutes until golden.

Freeze for up to 3 months. Defrost in the fridge overnight and reheat thoroughly.

Variation: pasticcio

Omit the aubergine. Boil 350g macaroni in lightly salted water until tender. Make the mince as above, spoon into a deep baking dish and top with the macaroni. Spoon the cheese sauce over and bake at 180°C/160°C fan/gas 4 for 35 minutes until golden.

Marcus Wareing's mini moussaka

Marcus Wareing creates the most amazing Michelin-starred food for his restaurant at The Berkeley hotel in Knightsbridge. But at the other end of the scale he can also create delicious down-to-earth homely dishes like this comforting moussaka for his young family.

Serves 4 | Takes 30 minutes to make, 15 minutes to cook

**4 small aubergines
2 tbsp vegetable oil
1 onion, sliced
2 cloves garlic, crushed
1 tsp ground cumin
1 tsp ground coriander
400g minced lamb
2 tablespoons tomato purée
1 tbsp soy sauce
250ml chicken stock
leaves from 1 sprig fresh rosemary
50g butter
50g flour
250ml milk
1 nutmeg, grated
25g Cheddar cheese, grated**

Set the oven to 180°C/160°C fan/gas 4. Wrap the aubergines individually in tin foil and place in the oven for 15 minutes. Remove and allow to cool for 20 minutes.

Heat a medium-sized frying pan over a moderate heat, add the oil, then the onions and garlic when hot. Fry lightly, then add the spices and the mince. Fry the mince until lightly browned then add the tomato purée, soy sauce, stock and rosemary. Allow to simmer gently.

Slice one edge off each aubergine and scrape out some of the flesh, leaving a good centimetre of flesh on the skin to allow the aubergine to hold its shape. Add the scraped flesh to the pan of lamb mince.

Make a béchamel sauce in a medium-sized saucepan by melting the butter then stirring in the flour. Slowly add the milk and mix well, adding the nutmeg and seasoning. Cook out for 10 minutes then add the cheese and adjust the seasoning if necessary.

The lamb mince should by now be relatively thick, if not, allow to reduce down further. Fill the cavity of the aubergine with the mince mix then spoon over a little of the béchamel sauce.

Serve immediately or wrap the stuffed aubergines in foil and set the béchamel aside until you are ready to serve. To reheat the aubergines, place in an oven set to 180°C/160°C fan/gas 4 for 10–15 minutes.

Not suitable for freezing.

Middle Eastern flatbreads with minced lamb

I first tasted these about 20 years ago when living near Stoke Newington in North London. There were many Middle Eastern delis along Green Lanes that served divine flatbreads topped with spinach and egg or spicy minced meat. They would be sold rolled up in greaseproof paper as perfect street food. This is a quick version which doesn't do justice to the original, but is very tasty nonetheless. For a really quick cheat, just make the topping and spread over readymade flatbreads. The lemon juice added at the end makes all the difference to the flavour so don't miss it out!

**Makes 8 flatbreads |
Takes 30 minutes to make,
15 minutes to cook**

For the flatbread dough
350g strong plain flour
1 tsp salt
2 tsp easy-blend yeast
250ml warm water
2 tbsp extra virgin olive oil

For the topping
1 small onion, halved
$1/2$ red or green pepper, deseeded
small handful fresh parsley
2 cloves garlic, crushed
250g minced lamb
1 tsp ground cumin
1 tsp ground coriander
good pinch cayenne pepper
2 tbsp natural yoghurt
2 tbsp pine nuts
1 tbsp raisins
juice of $1/2$ lemon

To make the dough, place the flour, salt and yeast into a bowl. Pour on the warm water and olive oil and mix to make a soft dough. Place on a floured work surface and knead until smooth and elastic. Return to the bowl and cover with clingfilm while making the mince topping.

Place the onion, pepper, parsley and garlic into a food processor and whizz until finely chopped. Place the vegetables in a bowl with the mince, spices, yoghurt, pine nuts and raisins and mix well.

Set the oven to 240°C/220°C fan/gas 9. Divide the dough into 8 portions. On a floured work surface, roll each piece of dough as thinly as possible into oval shapes about the size of a pitta bread. Place 2 on a baking tray and spread with the mince mixture. Bake for 14–15 minutes until the dough is risen and the meat is browned. Repeat with remaining mixture.

Drizzle each cooked flatbread with lemon juice before serving.

Not suitable for freezing.

Spanish pork, chorizo and bean soup

This is the kind of soup I like for lunch when working at home, or on a cold winter's evening. It is ideal for packed lunches – pour it, boiling hot, into a thermos flask and take to work with you.

Serves 4–6 | Takes 20 minutes to make, 40 minutes to cook

250g minced pork
75g chorizo sausage, chopped
1 stick celery, diced
1 onion, finely chopped
1 carrot, diced
1 cloves garlic, crushed
1 sprig rosemary, leaves stripped
   and chopped
1 tsp sweet smoked paprika
400g can chopped tomatoes
300ml vegetable or chicken stock
400g can cannelloni beans,
   drained
100g kale, shredded

Dry-fry the minced pork and chorizo in a large pan until browned. Add the celery, onion and carrot and cook over a low heat for 10 minutes until tender.

Add the garlic, rosemary and paprika. Cook for 1–2 minutes, then add the tomatoes, stock and beans. Bring up to the boil and simmer for 10 minutes. Add the kale, cook for 3–4 minutes then serve in bowls with crusty bread.

Can be frozen for up to 1 month.

Giancarlo's meat ragu

I have been to Giancarlo and Katie Caldesi's cookery school (Cucina Caldesi) and restaurants several times and have always enjoyed their food. Like all Italian chefs, Giancarlo is very passionate about his family ragu recipe which was passed down from his father's mother. The mince has the longest cooking time for any recipe in the book, but Giancarlo would not hear of cooking it for any shorter length of time! He knows it is ready just by smelling it at the beginning, halfway through and at the end of the cooking time and makes all his students smell it during cooking too. This recipe comes from their BBC book, *Return to Tuscany*.

Serves 8 | Takes 20 minutes to prepare, about 3 hours to cook

150ml extra-virgin olive oil
1½ red onions (about 150g), very finely chopped
2 celery sticks, (about 150g), very finely chopped
1 medium carrot (about 150g), very finely chopped
salt and freshly ground black pepper
2 sprigs fresh rosemary
3 bay leaves
2 cloves garlic, left whole and crushed with the flat side of a knife
750g minced beef
300g minced pork
400ml red wine
100ml chicken or beef stock plus extra if necessary
2 x 400g cans chopped tomatoes

Heat the olive oil in a large pan and add the onion, celery and carrot, and season with salt and pepper. Add the rosemary, bay leaves and garlic and cook over a low heat for 15 minutes, stirring often – this allows the onion to become sweet.

Remove the rosemary and bay leaves, then add the beef and pork mince and continue to cook until all the liquid from the meat has been absorbed. Keep stirring so that the mince doesn't stick to the bottom. When no more liquid is left add the wine and stir well. Sniff the sauce to see how strong the wine smells – it will change when it is cooked. Simmer over a low heat, uncovered, for 45 minutes.

Warm the stock to avoid lowering the temperature of the ragu and add it to the pan with the tomatoes. Stir well. At this point you'll be able to smell a wonderful mixture of flavours – first the tomatoes, then the meat, then the wine.

Leave uncovered and simmer for about 2 hours. Top up the level of liquid with a little more warm stock if the ragu starts to dry out. Taste and adjust the seasoning if necessary. At the end of the cooking time, smell the ragu again – no single ingredient should dominate. Serve with spaghetti.

Use the ragu straight away or cool and transfer to plastic containers for freezing. Use within 3 months.

Baked venison ragu with polenta

A hearty rich dish perfect for entertaining, this ragu is just as good made with minced beef and served with pappardelle.

Serves 6 | Takes 30 minutes to make, 40 minutes to cook

25g dried porcini mushrooms
300g coarse polenta
salt and freshly ground black pepper
2 tbsp rapeseed oil
400g minced venison
1 onion, chopped
3 cloves garlic, crushed
150g chestnut mushrooms,
400g can chopped tomatoes
150ml red wine
1 sprig fresh rosemary, chopped
1 sprig thyme, chopped
butter, for greasing
50g Parmesan cheese, grated

Place the dried porcini mushrooms into a small bowl and cover with boiling water for 30 minutes, then drain.

Line a large baking tray, about 1.5cm deep with clingfilm. In a large saucepan, bring 1.2 litres of salted water to the boil. Reduce the heat to low then slowly sprinkle in the polenta, whisking all the time to prevent lumps from forming. Cook gently for 8–10 minutes, stirring continuously until really thick. Remove from the heat, taste and season. Pour polenta into the baking tray and spread flat. Allow to cool.

Meanwhile, heat the oil in a medium shallow pan and fry the venison and onion for 5 minutes until browned. Add the garlic, drained porcini and chestnut mushrooms and fry for another 2–3 minutes, then pour over the tomatoes and the red wine and stir in the herbs. Season well and bring to the boil. Cover and simmer for 15 minutes.

Turn out the cold polenta and remove the clingfilm. Using a 5cm plain cutter, cut into circles.

Grease a deep 2-litre ovenproof dish with butter. Arrange the trimmings and half the circles of polenta in the base and sprinkle with half of the Parmesan. Pour over the venison sauce. Top with the remaining circles of polenta and sprinkle with the rest of the Parmesan.

Bake at 180°C/160°C fan/gas 4 for 40 minutes until golden brown and bubbling.

Freeze for up to 3 months. Defrost overnight in the fridge and reheat thoroughly.

VENISON

Berbere sauce

Every home in Ethiopia makes their own variation of a berbere spice mix for flavouring stews, casseroles and meat dishes. You need a heady mixture of spices but the end result is a rich, spicy supper that is well worth the effort. Use less chilli if you prefer a mild heat.

Serves 4 | Takes 10 minutes to make, 30 minutes to cook

1 tsp cumin seeds
10 cardamom pods, crushed
$^1/_2$ tsp fenugreek seeds, crushed
$^1/_2$ tsp coriander seeds,
4 cloves
$^1/_4$ tsp crushed dried chillies
$^1/_4$ tsp ground turmeric
$^1/_4$ tsp ground cinnamon
2 tsp sweet paprika
1 tsp mixed spice
2.5cm piece root ginger, grated
15g butter
1 onion, finely diced
500g minced lamb
400g can chopped tomatoes
salt and freshly ground black pepper
steamed couscous, to serve

In a small frying pan, dry-fry the cumin seeds, cardamom pods, fenugreek, coriander seeds and cloves gently for 2 minutes, stirring constantly. As soon as they start to jump or pop in the pan, remove from the heat and place in a pestle and mortar to crush them. Add the remaining spices and ginger.

Melt the butter in a large non-stick pan and cook the onion until lightly browned. Add the ginger and spices and cook for 1–2 minutes. Add the mince and cook for a further 5 minutes until brown.

Stir in the tomatoes and season with salt and pepper. Bring to the boil then reduce the heat, cover and cook for 20 minutes. Serve with steamed couscous.

Freeze sauce for up to 1 month. Defrost overnight in the fridge and reheat thoroughly until piping hot.

Golabki

This recipe – Polish stuffed cabbage leaves – was given to me by a Polish friend whose mother used to make this on an almost weekly basis for the family. You can vary the filling – instead of bacon, add chopped *cabanos* sausages or Polish smoked sausage. You can also serve the cabbage leaves with a rich tomato pasta sauce if you prefer.

Serves 6 | Takes 45 minutes to make, 1 hour to cook

1 medium Savoy cabbage
2 tbsp white wine vinegar
2 rashers smoked streaky bacon, chopped
500g lean minced pork or use half pork and half veal
2 onions, finely chopped
1 carrot, finely diced
1 red pepper, finely diced
200g long-grain rice
1 tbsp tomato purée
1 tsp salt
$\frac{1}{2}$ tsp freshly ground black pepper
1 tbsp chopped fresh parsley
200ml chicken stock
crème fraîche, to serve

Carefully peel away the cabbage leaves, cutting through the stalk to remove them from the central core. You will need 12 large, whole leaves. Place them in a large pan of boiling water with the vinegar and boil for 3–4 minutes until just softened. Drain well.

In a medium pan dry-fry the bacon, pork and onions for 5 minutes until the meat has browned and the onions are beginning to soften. Add the carrot and red pepper and continue to cook for another 5 minutes. Add the rice and tomato purée, stir and season well with the salt and pepper. Stir in the parsley.

Set the oven to 180°C/160°C fan/gas 4.

Lay one leaf at a time on a worksurface and add a good spoonful of the mince mixture towards the stem end, roll up from the stem, folding in the sides of the cabbage to ensure the filling is tightly wrapped. Repeat with the remaining cabbage and filling. Place the cabbage rolls seam side down in a large shallow baking dish and pour over the stock. Cover with a tight fitting lid and bake in the oven for 1 hour or until tender. Serve with crème fraîche.

Not suitable for freezing.

Crispy stir-fried pork with lemongrass and chillies

This is a fast, tasty supper with a piquant sauce and fine noodles, a perfect pick-me-up supper. Make sure you drain off the fat or you will end up with stewed pork rather than crispy pork.

Serves 4 | Takes 10 minutes to make, 10 minutes to cook

4 tbsp Thai fish sauce (nam pla)
juice 2 limes
2 tbsp muscovado sugar
1 tbsp sesame oil
500g minced pork
$^1/_2$ onion, finely diced
1 lemongrass stalk, finely chopped
$^1/_2$ red chilli, finely chopped
2 cloves garlic, crushed
2 spring onions, sliced
cellophane or glass noodles, to serve
handful shredded coriander, to garnish

Make the sauce by mixing together the Thai fish sauce, lime juice, muscovado sugar and sesame oil.

Heat a large frying pan or wok and fry the pork and onion for 10 minutes until browned then place in a sieve to drain off the excess fat. Return the mince to the pan and continue to fry the pork for another 5 minutes or until golden and crispy. Add the lemongrass, chilli and garlic and fry for 2–3 minutes then add the sauce and spring onions. Heat through and serve with the cooked noodles and garnish with the coriander.

Not suitable for freezing.

PORK

Chinese pork-fried rice

This is one of the quickest recipes in the book and a great last-minute supper if you have cooked leftover rice.

**Serves 4 | Takes 5 minutes
to make, 15 minutes to cook**

**200g minced pork
400g cooked basmati rice
200g frozen peas
3 eggs, beaten
2 tbsp light soy sauce
8 spring onions, trimmed and
   sliced
1 tsp sesame oil**

Dry-fry the pork in a large frying pan for about 10 minutes until browned and tender. Add the rice and peas, fry for about 3–4 minutes until hot, then pour on the beaten egg. Stir over the heat for just a minute or so until the egg is lightly scrambled. Add the soy sauce, spring onions, and sesame oil, toss together and serve straight away.

Not suitable for freezing.

Thai butternut chicken curry

A simple, quick, warming, spicy supper.

**Serves 4 | Takes 20 minutes
to make, 25 minutes to cook**

2 tbsp sunflower oil
250g butternut squash, cut into
  chunks
1 onion, chopped
250g minced chicken or turkey
2 tbsp Thai green curry paste
50g creamed coconut
100g mangetout peas
100g baby sweetcorn, halved
boiled rice, to serve

Heat the oil in a large pan and fry the butternut squash and onion for 5 minutes. Add the chicken or turkey and fry for a further 5 minutes until browned.

Add the Thai curry paste and cook for 1 minute then add the creamed coconut and 300ml water. Bring to the boil, and simmer for 10–15 minutes until the squash is tender.

Add the mangetout and sweetcorn, and cook for a further 5 minutes. Serve with boiled rice.

Not suitable for freezing.

South African bobotie

This recipe was given to me by Jacqui, a South African friend, who used to eat this whenever she went back home to visit her grandmother. The recipe was lost but over the years she has tracked down and tried many variations and has now fine tuned it to this. It is the national dish of South Africa, a little like shepherd's pie but with delicious African spicing.

Serves 4–6 | Takes 15 minutes to make, 30–40 minutes to cook

25g butter
1 onion, finely chopped
500g minced beef
2 cloves garlic, crushed
2 tsp garam masala
1/2 tsp turmeric
1 tsp ground cumin
1 tsp ground coriander
1/2 tsp ground cinnamon
1/2 tsp mixed spice
1 tsp mixed dried herbs
small handful fresh parsley, chopped
50g sultanas
50g ready-to-eat dried apricots, chopped
1 eating apple, diced
25g flaked almonds
3 tbsp fruity brown sauce

For the topping
3 eggs
250ml milk
pinch ground nutmeg

Set the oven to 180°C/160°C fan/gas 4.

Heat the butter in a large saucepan and very gently fry the onion until softened, but not browned. Add the mince and fry until it is browned all over. Add the garlic, spices and herbs. Stir in the sultanas, apricots, apple and almonds and fruity brown sauce. Transfer the mixture to a large 1-litre ovenproof dish.

Beat the eggs into the milk and pour over the top. Sprinkle with nutmeg. Bake for 30–40 minutes until the custard topping has set and is golden brown.

Not suitable for freezing.

Pad Thai noodles

Traditionally this is made with tiger prawns but minced chicken or turkey works well. If liked, you can also use straight to wok, pre-cooked noodles.

Serves 2 | Takes 5 minutes to make, 12 minutes to cook

250g rice noodles
2 tbsp sunflower oil
200g minced chicken or turkey
1 clove garlic, crushed
1 egg, beaten
1 red chilli, thinly sliced
1 carrot, grated
200g beansprouts
1 tbsp brown sugar
3 tbsp Thai fish sauce (nam pla)
zest and juice 1 lime
50g salted peanuts
3 spring onions, sliced

If using dried rice noodles, soak them in a bowl of boiling water for 10 minutes until softened, then drain and set to one side.

Heat the oil in a wok or large frying pan and stir-fry the chicken or turkey for 8–10 minutes until well cooked. Add the garlic, cook for a minute then add the beaten egg and cook, stirring until lightly scrambled. Add the chilli, cooked noodles, carrot, beansprouts, brown sugar, fish sauce and lime juice and cook for 1–2 minutes until piping hot. Sprinkle with the peanuts and spring onions. Serve hot or cold.

Not suitable for freezing.

Balti beef curry with fragrant rice

A fast easy midweek meal.

Serves 4 | Takes 10 minutes to make, 20 minutes to cook

For the rice
350g basmati rice
1 small cinnamon stick, crumbled
8 green cardamom pods, cracked

For the balti
1 tbsp sunflower oil
3cm piece fresh root ginger, chopped
1 clove garlic, crushed
500g minced beef
1 red onion, sliced
2–3 tbsp balti curry paste
6 tomatoes, chopped
handful fresh spinach
fresh coriander, to garnish

Cook the rice, cinnamon stick and cardamom pods in salted, boiling water for 12 minutes until fluffy (when cooked, remove the cinnamon stick and cardamom pods).

Meanwhile, heat the oil in a large frying pan or wok. Add the ginger and garlic and fry for 1 minute, add the minced beef and onion and fry for 3–4 minutes until beef is browned all over. Add the balti paste, tomatoes and 4 tablespoons of boiling water. Cook for 10–15 minutes adding a little extra water to make a saucy consistency if necessary. Add the spinach, stir and cook for 2 minutes until the spinach has wilted. Serve with the rice and coriander to garnish.

Freeze for up to 1 month. Defrost overnight in the fridge and reheat thoroughly.

Keema curry

This is quite a dry curry, delicious served with naan bread, rice or even stuffed into tomatoes and baked.

Serve 4 | Takes 5 minutes to make, 30 minutes to cook

1 tbsp sunflower oil
2 onions, thinly sliced
2 cloves garlic, crushed
2cm piece fresh root ginger, grated
1 tbsp ground cumin
2 tsp ground coriander
$1/4$ tsp chilli powder
$1/4$ tsp turmeric
500g minced lamb
4 tomatoes, chopped
100g frozen peas
1 tbsp chopped fresh coriander leaves
1 tbsp chopped fresh mint
1 tbsp lemon juice
salt and freshly ground black pepper
rice and naan bread, to serve

Heat the oil in a medium saucepan and fry the onions for about 10 minutes until tender and just beginning to colour. Add the garlic, ginger and spices and cook over a low heat for 1–2 minutes to release their fragrance. Add the lamb and fry until browned all over.

Add the tomatoes, taste and season with salt and pepper if needed. Reduce the heat to low, cover and let the mince cook for 15 minutes. Add the peas, coriander, mint and lemon juice and heat through. Serve hot with rice and naan bread.

Freeze for up to 1 month. Defrost overnight in the fridge and reheat thoroughly.

Keema naan bread

These are a great accompaniment to a curry or delicious to eat on their own.

Makes 6 breads | Takes about 1 hour to prepare, 10 minutes to cook

675g strong white bread flour
1$\frac{1}{2}$ tsp salt
75g butter
25g caster sugar
1 sachet easy blend dried yeast
450ml milk
15g ghee or melted butter

For the filling
100g minced lamb
$\frac{1}{2}$ small onion, chopped
$\frac{1}{2}$ tsp ground cumin
good pinch garam masala
pinch salt
2 tbsp raisins

To make the naan, mix together the flour and salt and rub in the butter until it looks like breadcrumbs. Stir in the sugar and yeast. Make a well in the centre and add the milk. Mix to a dough then turn out on a well floured work surface and knead for 10 minutes until smooth. Place in a bowl and cover with oiled clingfilm and leave in a warm place until doubled in size.

Meanwhile, dry-fry the lamb with the onion until browned all over. Add the cumin and garam masala and season with a little salt. Stir in the raisins and leave to cool.

When the dough has doubled in size, turn it out of the bowl and knead lightly. Cut the dough into 6 equal pieces. Roll out each piece thinly to a round shape. Place a spoonful of lamb mixture in the centre and bring the sides up to the centre to cover the meat. Pinch well then turn over and roll out the bread to a thin flat round.

Set the grill to high and warm a baking sheet underneath. Make fork holes all over each piece of bread and place on the baking tray. Place the tray under the grill but not too close and grill for a few minutes each side until brown patches appear. Remove from the grill, brush with melted butter or ghee and keep warm in the oven until needed.

Not suitable for freezing.

Rick Stein's Shepherd's pie as cooked in India

This recipe, from *Rick Stein's Food Heroes; Another Helping* (BBC Books), is one that Rick recalls from his childhood when his mother used to make a dry lamb curry and often turn it into a Raj-style shepherd's pie. It was always served with sweet mango chutney. It is now the kind of meal he likes to serve to friends for an informal supper.

Serves 4–6 | Takes 55 minutes to make, 35 minutes to cook

2 tbsp sunflower oil
1 onion, finely chopped
4 garlic cloves, crushed
2.5cm piece root ginger, grated
900g lean minced lamb
1 small red chilli, deseeded and
   finely chopped
1 tsp ground turmeric
1 tbsp ground coriander
1 tbsp ground cumin
1 vine-ripened tomato, chopped
1 tbsp tomato purée
1 tsp tamarind paste
300ml chicken stock
handful fresh coriander leaves,
   chopped
salt and freshly ground black
   pepper

For the mash
1.25kg floury potatoes (such as
   King Edward), cut into chunks
50g butter
a little full-fat milk

Heat the oil in a large pan, add the onion, garlic and ginger and fry over a medium heat until the onion is soft and just beginning to brown. Add the minced lamb, chilli, turmeric, ground coriander and cumin and fry until the meat is lightly browned.

Stir in the chopped tomato, tomato purée, tamarind paste and stock. Season with salt and pepper and simmer for 30 minutes, until the mixture has thickened but is still nice and moist.

Meanwhile, place the potatoes in a large saucepan of salted water, bring to the boil, then simmer until tender. Drain and allow to cool slightly, then pass through a potato ricer (or mash with a potato masher). Return the potato to the pan, then beat in the butter and season with salt and pepper. Add just enough milk to form a soft, spreadable mash.

Set the oven to 200°C/180°C fan/gas 6.

Stir the coriander leaves into the lamb, then transfer the mixture to a shallow 1.75-litre ovenproof dish.

Spoon the potato topping over the lamb mixture and mark the surface with a fork. Place in the oven for 30–35 minutes or until the surface is golden brown.

Freeze for up to 3 months. Defrost overnight and reheat thoroughly.

Indian-style Scotch eggs

I have come across several rather complicated but delicious sounding Indian Scotch eggs which use venison mince and lots of different curry spices, the Scotch eggs are then cooked or served with a curry sauce. Being a working mum, I've rarely the time to cook Indian meals from scratch so I've come up with a quick cheats version of this dish, and I've served them cold rather than cooking them in a sauce.

Makes 6 | Takes 20 minutes to make, 30 minutes to cook

6 eggs
250g good quality pork sausages
450g minced game
1 clove garlic, crushed
2 tbsp chopped fresh coriander
1 tsp garam masala
$\frac{1}{4}$ tsp ground cumin
$\frac{1}{4}$ tsp ground coriander
1 tsp salt
1 tsp black pepper
2 tbsp instant polenta or cornmeal
1 tbsp sunflower oil, for frying
mango chutney, to serve

Bring a pan of water to the boil, add the eggs and boil for 7–8 minutes. Drain, plunge the eggs in cold water and, when cool, remove the shells.

Slip the skins off the sausages and place in a mixing bowl with the minced game. Add the garlic, coriander, spices and seasoning and mix well. You can fry a little of the mixture in a tablespoon of hot vegetable oil until cooked, then taste and adjust the seasoning if necessary. Set the oven to 220°C/200°C fan/gas 7.

Divide the mince mixture into 6 pieces. Roll each into a large ball, flatten and wrap around an egg, squeezing the mixture well around the egg to make sure it is enclosed. Roll the egg in the polenta then place on a baking tray and bake for 30 minutes until the meat is cooked. Serve cold with mango chutney.

Not suitable for freezing.

Chinese pork buns

I always like to look for a quick way to make tasty meals and these Chinese buns are no exception. I love the *Char Sui* buns (or roast pork buns) that you get in Chinese dim sum restaurants, so although not as good, my buns have a sweet sticky pork filling that is quite delicious. These are great as a starter to a Chinese meal or as a canapé to hand around at parties. They can be made in advance and chilled until ready to cook.

Makes 12 buns | Takes 20 minutes to make, 10–12 mins to cook

250g minced pork
2 tsp fresh root ginger, grated
1 clove garlic
1 tbsp teriyaki marinade
1 tsp sesame oil
2 tsp light soy sauce
500g puff pastry
1 egg white
1 tbsp sesame seeds
flour, for dusting

In a frying pan, dry-fry the minced pork for about 5 minutes until browned. Place the pork in a sieve to drain off the fat and return to the pan. Continue to cook over a very high heat for another 5 minutes until the pork browns and begins to caramelise, stirring occasionally to prevent it sticking to the pan. Add the ginger and garlic, fry for 1 minute, then add the teriyaki marinade and soy sauce. Tip the mixture onto a plate to help it cool down quickly.

Set the oven to 220°C/210°C fan/gas 7.

Dust the worksurface with flour and roll out the pastry thinly and cut out 24 circles, using a pastry cutter, 8cm in diameter. Spoon a little mixture into the centre of 12 of the pastry circles. Brush the edges with a little water and place the other 12 circles on top. Press well to seal the edges and prevent them popping open when cooked. Brush the tops with egg white and sprinkle with sesame seeds. Bake for 10–12 minutes until golden brown. Serve warm from the oven.

Freeze uncooked. Cook from frozen allowing an extra 5 minutes cooking time or until reheated thoroughly.

A

B

British and American cookbooks use different measuring systems. In the UK, dry ingredients are measured by weight, with the metric system increasingly replacing the Imperial one, while in the US they are measured by volume.

Weight

7g	¼ ounce	200g	7 ounces
20g	¾ ounce	220–225g	8 ounces
25–30g	1 ounce	250–260g	9 ounces
40g	1½ ounces	300g	10½ ounces
50g	1¾ ounces	325g	11½ ounces
60–65g	2¼ ounces	350g	12 ounces
70–75g	2½ ounces	400g	14 ounces
80g	2¾ ounces	450g	1 pound
90g	3¼ ounces	500g	1 pound 2 ounces
100g	3½ ounces	600g	1 pound 5 ounces
110–115g	4 ounces	700g	1 pound 9 ounces
120–130g	4½ ounces	750g	1 pound 10 ounces
140g	5 ounces	800g	1¾ pounds
150g	5½ ounces	900g	2 pounds
175–180g	6 ounces	1kg	2¼ pounds

Volume

50ml	1¾ fl oz	300ml	10 fl oz
60ml	2 fl oz (4 tablespoons/¼ cup)	350ml	12 fl oz
75ml	2½ fl oz (5 tablespoons)	400ml	14 fl oz
90ml	3 fl oz (⅜ cup)	450ml	15 fl oz
100ml	3½ fl oz	475ml	16 fl oz (2 cups)
125ml	4 fl oz (½ cup)	500ml	18 fl oz
150ml	5 fl oz (⅔ cup)	600ml	20 fl oz
175ml	6 fl oz	800ml	28 fl oz
200ml	7 fl oz	850ml	30 fl oz
250ml	8 fl oz (1 cup)	1 litre	35 fl oz (4 cups)

Length

5mm	¼ inch	8cm	3¼ inches
1cm	½ inch	9cm	3½ inches
2cm	¾ inch	10cm	4 inches
2.5cm	1 inch	12cm	4½ inches
3cm	1¼ inches	14cm	5½ inches
4cm	1½ inches	20cm	8 inches
5cm	2 inches	24cm	9½ inches
6cm	2½ inches	30cm	12 inches

MEASURES